The Creative Journal

The CREATIVE JOURNAL

The ART OF FINDING YOURSELF

BY LUCIA CAPACCHIONE

Swallow Press
ATHENS
OHIO UNIVERSITY PRESS

Swallow Press books are published by Ohio University Press.
Swallow Press/Ohio University Press books are printed on acid-free paper. ∞

First edition
Fifth printing, 1985.
Sixth printing, 1987.
Seventh printing, 1989

LIBRARY OF CONGRESS CATALOG CARD NUMBER: 78-51590
ISBN 0-8040-0798-5

Acknowledgements

Illustrations, both drawn and written, are from the journals of students in my Creative Journal classes:

Felice Bachrach	Star Jenkins
Robin Baltic	Joyce King
Regina Barton	Jane Murphy
Victoria Becker	Mary Jane Maier
Elaine Bourne	Celia Pearce
Gary Brown	Carole Petracca
Lucia Capacchione	Ruth Randle
Albert Cirimele	Carroll Shupe
Jane Kelly Corns	Suzanne Stokes
Bill Eidelman	Jennifer Svendsen
Lucille Isenberg	Marge Windish

My deepest thanks to you all and to *all* the students, past and future, who make the class such a joy for me.

My gratitude also to the Santa Monica YWCA and its director, Beverly Sanborn, who believed in the Creative Journal course and helped it to be born. And thanks to Los Angeles City College Community Services for sponsoring my workshops.

Cover and book design: Lucia Capacchione
Photography: Michael Jones

Dedicated
to
Anaïs Nin
who
inspired me
to keep a journal
in the first place

Contents

The Creative Journal

1 What Is Creative Journal-Keeping?

How it all began

My own journal was born during a period of personal crisis. I had come to a dead-end after going through a rapid series of major changes. In four years I had gotten a divorce, moved four times, and had several different free-lance jobs as a design and education consultant. I was also raising two young daughters.

I know now that the fruits of serious self-reflection cannot be measured. But self-exploration takes time, solitude, and courage. It can be very painful. I had survived several crisis-filled years and managed to postpone my confrontation with myself. But the stress of coping with all those changes finally caught up with me and, in 1973, I became ill and unable to work for many weeks. I was filled with confusion about my career direction as well as my personal life. The time had come to stop and reflect.

When I became ill, the years of pain and confusion loomed up like some primitive monster of the deep. I had to face "the monster" or drown. There were many nights when I thought I was going under for the last time. I lived in fear of dying. The strange paradox is that by confronting my fear of death, I found myself and created a new life.

As I sat in bed wondering how and why I was going to get well, I had lots of time to puzzle about my life. I did a lot of reading and drawing. I read C.G. Jung's *Man and His Symbols* and the first four volumes of Anaïs Nin's *Diary*. These books were to have a profound effect on my art, my work with people, and my life in general.

I was especially touched by Anaïs Nin's words and felt that she was speaking directly to me. Reading her *Diary* I saw that the journal could be an excellent tool for revealing the Self to oneself in the service of personal growth. So I began keeping a journal and there I experienced the consolation of release.

2 My journal started as a written record of my innermost feelings and thoughts, a dialog with myself. Within a few months, I developed the awareness and the courage to go into psychotherapy for the first time. Shortly after entering therapy, I began to come back to life and, as I continued regaining energy and health, my inner movement was reflected in the journal pages. I began to draw, to write poetry, to integrate words and images in patterns that flowed across the page. Pages that had been filled with neat little rows of handwritten prose were now bursting with poetic and graphic records of my travels to inner space. I was alive and well and expressing myself in a new way. Plates 1 and 2.

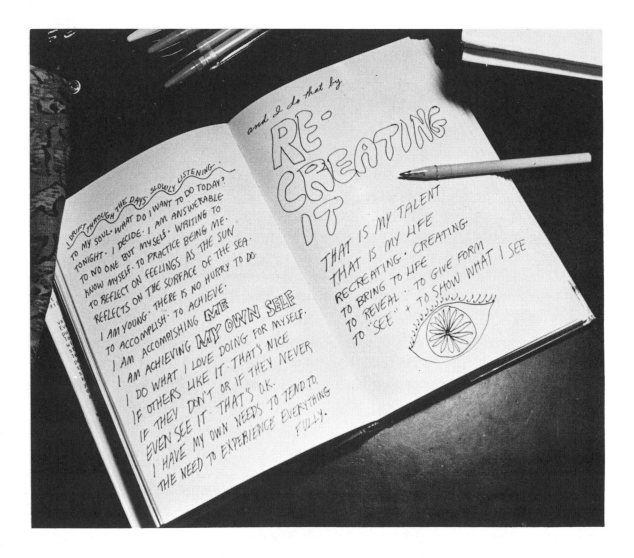

Plate 1   Photo: Jim Ruebsamen, Santa Monica *Evening Outlook*

3

Photo: Jim Ruebsamen, Santa Monica *Evening Outlook*   Plate 2

4 As I continued pouring myself out into the journal, I was spontaneously coming up with techniques which heightened awareness, aided the self-inventory process, and helped break through many blocks. In the first year of journal-keeping, I moved from the darkest depression through a gray cloud of confusion to emerge eventually into the sunlight. As my inner eye grew accustomed to the light, I could see my future and walk eagerly toward it. *I had died and been reborn.*

One year and a half after beginning the journal, I entered graduate school in psychology and went into the field of art therapy where I combined my training and experience as an artist/teacher with a passionate concern for human growth. Of course, I continued to use art as therapy in my own journal, developing more exercises focusing on feelings, thoughts, wishes, and plans.

While I was in graduate school, I met many people who were keeping journals. With what excitement they spoke of the value of the journal process for personal growth! Some of them had been inspired by Anaïs Nin's *Diary,* as I had. I felt a deep sense of connection with all these journal-keepers who were quietly exploring themselves in solitude and tapping into vast storehouses of hidden dreams and creative potential.

I began to include journal exercises into my art therapy groups and creativity workshops. At these workshops, the diarists came crawling out of the woodwork, hungry for ideas on how to use their journals more productively for creative self-development. Encouraged by the enthusiastic response I was getting, I put together a course called, *The Creative Journal: Finding the Buried Treasure Within.* My first class was sponsored by the Y.W.C.A. in Santa Monica. We met in small groups, did exercises together, and shared our reactions and questions. We used our journals for releasing feelings, doing self-assessment, career and life-goal planning, confidence-building, and creative expression in words and graphic art. Above all, we were developing and strengthening our self-esteem and creative power and that was most heartening for me. The class was very successful and I have continued teaching it privately and at various colleges and other institutions.

I also lead workshops for special interest groups, such as therapists, vocational counselors, teachers wishing to use the journal for their own growth and also incorporate it into their professional work.

What is Creative Journal-keeping?

Creative Journal-keeping is a tool for personal growth using journal writing and drawing. As a guide to Creative Journal-keeping, this book contains a series of exercises designed to help you find and love your own *dear self*. The exercises can help you:

- express feelings and thoughts
- play with new media of expression (color, images, symbols)
- sort out the seemingly random experiences in your life
- make more conscious choices and decisions
- define and implement changes
- get a clearer picture of your creative potential and how to use it
- deal with creative blocks and negative patterns
- enrich your relationship with yourself and others
- find deeper meaning in your life

The exercises are intended as a jumping-off point into your own growth and personal style of expression. I have arranged them in the general order they have been presented in my classes. This sequence has worked well for my students: starting with the known (present and past) and then looking at the unknown (the future which is yet to be shaped). However, once you have been through the exercises, you are encouraged to use them in any order that feels right to you. Go with your own mood and inclination. The table of contents lists the exercises by name and is a ready reference for locating the exercise that best serves your purpose at any given time.

In keeping a journal, many options are open to you. You can:

- modify or expand these exercises
- use exercises from other sources
- invent your own
- throw exercises to the wind and express yourself spontaneously

This is not a method, but an open-ended approach for you to play with. Your journal is a place to let yourself out, channel your private inner world into tangible form. The page becomes a mirror for seeing yourself more clearly. It is also a medium for conversing freely with yourself.

Starting with self-communication in private, you can then develop your ability to communicate with others. Being clear with yourself opens the way for being more clear with others about how you feel and think, enriching your relationships and social interactions.

I have included some examples of work done by my journal students. The sharing that happens in these groups is very beautiful and inspiring. I wanted to include you, the reader, in this sharing process. However, one note of caution. These journal illustrations are in no way meant to instruct you in "how to do the exercises." There are no shoulds or oughts, no one correct way. There is only your way. *Whatever feels right for you is the right way to do the exercises.* Elaborate on them or depart from them altogether. There are no rules here, only suggestions and ideas for you to try out. Explore and experiment. That's the way creative journal-keeping was born, that's how it will stay alive.

Forms of expression

The exercises are done through different forms of expression:

- drawings, doodles, and scribbles
- prose and poetry
- dramatic dialogs and letters
- graphs and charts
- colors, abstract designs, images, and symbols

If you think you're untalented or uncreative, some of these expressive forms might put you off. Take heart. You need no special talent or training in the arts to do these exercises. The goal is not to make art or literature, but to explore the self. You are not drawing or writing to please anyone else, to get approval or to meet externally imposed standards of aesthetics. Remember, the journal is by you for you. The only critic you have to deal with is yourself.

Granted, the fear of making something "ugly" can be great indeed, especially for adults who have done no spontaneous art since kindergarten. A sequence of pages from one man's journal clearly illustrates the point (Plates 3-8). After putting himself down for doing "ugly" scribbles, he finally broke through his block about drawing and was able to express some very deep feelings in a beautifully poignant drawing (Plate 9).

I like my journal. I like to be me. And noone can stop me.

*except me.

Plate 3

AND I WON'T LET ME STOP ME.

To prove it, I am going to express myself artistically on the next page.

I am getting nervous. It is not easy to stop me from preventing me from being me!

Plate 4

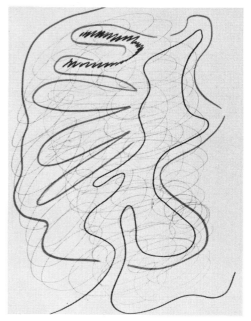

Plate 5

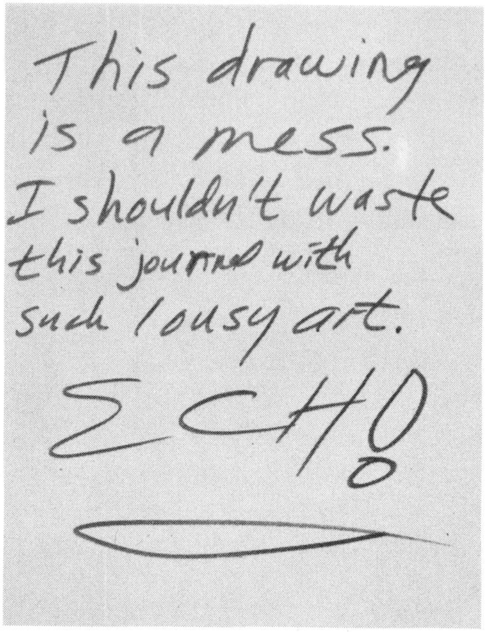

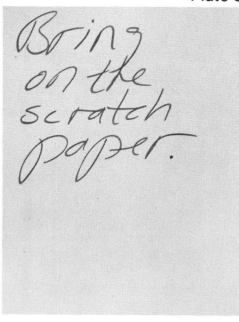

Plate 6

Plate 7

Plate 8

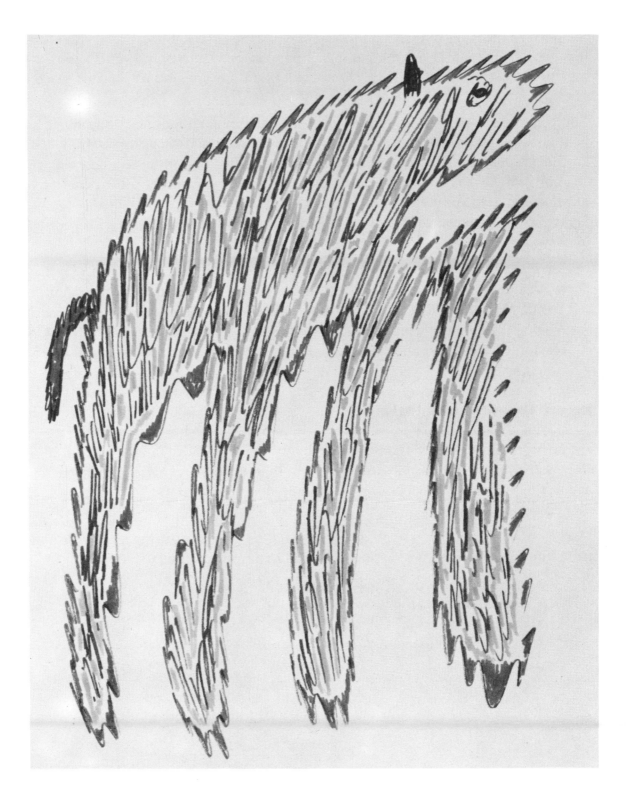

"I feel like a small, helpless, neglected animal crying for love and attention."

Plate 9

My hope is that you will relax and enjoy exploring colors, lines, shapes, textures, images, symbols, and words. Let your imagination out to play and discover your own unique style of expression. No one can find it for you and it is best learned by doing.

You may find that you enjoy drawing and creative writing once you have given yourself the chance to try it in a safe, non-judgemental atmosphere. Many of my journal students have discovered latent abilities in the arts, much to their surprise. Of course, if you are already an artist, poet, or writer you can certainly benefit from journal work. It is an excellent tool for sharpening sensitivities and awareness. Sketchbooks, diaries, and journals have been used for this purpose throughout history.

I offer *The Creative Journal* as a tool for your personal growth and development. Draw, write, or use whatever medium feels right for you. Listen to what's happening inside you and choose the exercise that seems to offer the best channel for expressing those inner feelings. Some feelings or states of being lend themselves to expression through visual arts, others flow more easily through words. It is up to you to choose.

Uses of Creative Journal-keeping

In the first volume of her *Diary* Anaïs Nin writes, "The diary taught me that it is in the moments of emotional crisis that human beings reveal themselves most accurately. I learned to choose the heightened moments because they are the moments of revelation."

Many journal-keepers report that they began their journals during a crisis or major transition. These times are usually marked by important events, such as:

- graduation from school
- seeking or starting a new career
- marriage or establishing a significant relationship
- birth of a child

- moving to a new location
- separation or divorce
- illness
- retirement
- death of a loved one

These events are often accompanied by deep feelings such as pain, loss, grieving, confusion, anger, fear, insecurity. At such times, a person is often compelled to do some serious soul-searching. This is when Creative Journal-keeping can be extremely helpful as a means for sorting out life experiences and feelings which seem overwhelming.

Of course, one does not have to be in a major or mini-crisis in order to benefit from journal exploration. For some, it is an essential part of the never-ending process of personal growth. It can be a place to express joy, excitement, and creative ideas as well as a place of refuge in the storm. As one student put it, "My journal has become my best friend. I can tell it anything."

Guidelines for Creative Journal-keeping

This book is intended as a guide, a road map for the inner journey to find yourself. It contains a series of exercises, each with its own descriptive title, theme, and purpose. I suggest that you familiarize yourself with these exercises by doing them once through in the order they appear. Experience them. Find out how they can work for you, what they can help you accomplish.

You will notice that each exercise is divided into sub-sections separated by black lines. I recommend that you do them one sub-section at a time, as follows:

1. Read the instructions in the first sub-section, stopping at the black line.
2. Do that sub-section of the exercise.

3. Go on to the next sub-section, read it, and follow the instructions.

4. Continue through each sub-section until you've completed the entire exercise.

After you have familiarized yourself with the exercises in this way, I encourage you to use the book in any sequence or manner you wish. Consider it a reference manual. Find the exercise that best suits your mood or need at the moment, using the table of contents as your guide. Let your inner voice lead you to the appropriate technique for exploring and expressing what is inside you. For instance, I have learned that when I am feeling self-critical and am doubting my own worth, I need to do the "Critical and Assertive Selves" exercise. For me personally, it always clears out those nagging self-put-downs that can be so debilitating. Many of my students report that when they have strong feelings but don't know what they are or what to do about them, they use the "How Am I Feeling" exercise. Simply expressing the feelings helps them experience more fully and does wonders in releasing and resolving pent-up emotions.

Regarding the form of the exercises themselves, there is nothing sacred about them. They are simply structures within which to improvise and use your own creativity. Feel free to use all or part of each exercise, to change it as you wish. Play around and adapt it to your needs. Make it your own.

Setting

The physical setting has an important effect upon journal work. I suggest finding a quiet, private place; one that is comfortable and conducive to meditation and self-reflection. You might want to settle into your favorite chair or other spot where you feel at home with yourself. The exercises are best done in an atmosphere of quiet concentration with no interferences or distractions from without. Reserve a block of uninterrupted time, fifteen minutes or more, depending upon how many exercises you wish to do at one sitting. Some take more time than others so you will need to take that into account.

Use your journal when you feel like it. Write or draw when:

- you have something to express
- you want to work with specific exercises
- you simply want to be alone with yourself

You may want to work in your journal every day, but that is not necessary, in my view. If you do work daily, you might want to set aside a regular time and place that is best for you. Personally, I find that just before bedtime is good, especially after a very busy day. It helps me put things into perspective and clear my mind before going to sleep. When my days are not so busy, I use my journal at different times as the impulse arises. I often carry it with me in a special journal bag and use it while waiting for appointments, travelling, or "killing time."

If you are working with dreams, it is important to write or draw them down as soon as you wake up so you don't forget them. You may not have time to de-code them in the morning, but at least you have the raw material documented for later use.

Spontaneity

Journal-keeping is a means of documenting the spontaneous flow of your life and growth. It is a vehicle for experiencing the present more fully and also witnessing past patterns and setting goals for the future. I recommend that you keep your journal as you live it. Date each entry sequentially and keep them in chronological order. This will enable you to later review your life experiences exactly as they unfolded.

Life doesn't happen in categories. It evolves organically and often mysteriously. For the sake of clarity as a reference guide, this book is divided into chapters and thematic topics. However, I do not mean to imply or suggest that you should keep your journal in categories or limit yourself to "exercise" work only. On the contrary, I urge you to flow with your own life and respond, in your journal, to experiences as they happen. The exercises are merely a tool for self-exploration and a spring-board into your own unique expression.

Creative Journal-keeping is intended for personal growth and development. Whether it works or not depends upon you and how willing you are to be honest with yourself. For this reason, it is advisable to keep your journal private and confidential. You will be more honest with yourself if you know that no one else will see your writing or drawing. It is difficult to be completely honest if you are worrying about how others will react. Protect your right to privacy. I recommend keeping your journal in a special place and not just leaving it about where others might pick it up and casually browse through. If you live with others, establish ground rules maintaining privacy for your journal work. You may want to store your completed volumes away in a special place and keep the current one in a carrying bag along with your pens and pencils.

Selective Sharing

If there are passages or drawings you wish to share, be selective about it. Share with people you trust, who are accepting of you. Avoid sharing with people who put you down, criticize, or tell you what you should or should not feel and think. Journal work does not flourish in a judgemental atmosphere. In fact, that's a good way to kill it.

It is helpful to find a friend who is also a journal-keeper so that you can engage in mutual sharing. Another journal-keeper may be more likely to understand what you are doing. Sharing journal work is like sharing secrets: it can bring people closer together. It's a way to exchange insights about ourselves and, through shared revelations, to see the human bond of universal feelings and experiences. Selective sharing counteracts the sense of isolation and makes travel into inner space less lonely.

Group sharing has been an important aspect of my journal classes. The groups are small, usually ten to fifteen people sitting in a circle. We normally meet in homes, lounges, or other informal settings to help establish a relaxed atmosphere. People are free to share or not share their work or reactions to the exercises. We are open and non-judgemental yet there is no group pressure to "tell all." This is not group therapy or encounter. We inspire and encourage one another and have developed wonderful support groups. Many friendships have been made, with others as well as the self. After you've experienced journal work for yourself, you might want to get a group of journal-keepers together for regular meetings using the exercises in this book as a springboard.

In my weekly course, each session is one-and-one-half to two hours long with a break in the middle. Each session begins with discussion about the last class or experiences during the intervening week. Sometimes we have done exercises for "homework" and will talk about these. Then we do the exercises together.

1. Choose an exercise and have one person read it aloud.
2. Quietly do the exercises with no talking. This can take from fifteen to twenty minutes, depending on the exercise.
3. Discuss any reactions to the exercise or share anything you wish from your journal.
4. Do another exercise, as described above, and repeat until the allotted time is over.

It is crucial that the tone of these sessions be non-judgemental and non-competitive, with absolutely no pressure to share or conform to any expectations from other individuals in the group.

Materials for Creative Journal-keeping

A notebook with plain white, unruled paper in a convenient size (6" x 9" or 8½" x 11") that is durable so pages won't tear or fall out easily.

I recommend one of the following:

a. A "blank book." This is a hardbound or paperback book with plain white pages, available in art supply, stationery or book stores.

b. A spiral-bound sketch pad, from art supply or stationery stores.

c. A three-ring loose-leaf folder with plain white paper, unlined. If you write more easily at the typewriter and want to type the verbal material in your journal, this is the book for you.

2. Tools for writing and drawing

The minimum is one set of fine point felt pens or colored pencils in eight assorted colors. Some other media are:

- medium or wide tip felt pens for drawing
- crayons
- oil or chalk pastels (use spray fixative with chalk pastels to prevent smearing or rubbing off.)

Preparing to Work in Your Journal

When you are ready to work in your journal, set aside a block of uninterrupted time of fifteen minutes or more. Gather your materials, notebook, and writing/drawing tools and settle down in the place you have chosen to be with yourself.

Relaxation

Creativity flows more naturally when you are relaxed, so it is helpful to become as relaxed as possible before you begin work. Use any relaxation technique you like. In my classes I suggest the following:

Close your eyes. Do some deep breathing. Slowly take the air in and let it out. Do this several times.

Now, focus in on the feelings inside your body. See if there are any areas of tension or pain. Do an inventory of your body. Start with your head and face. Move down to your neck and shoulders, then to your arms and hands. Check each area for tension. Then move down to your chest and abdomen, your back. Then your pelvic area and buttocks. Your thighs and knees, calves, and feet.

Go back to any areas of tension. Continue deep breathing and, as you exhale, allow the tense areas of your body to relax, one by one. Each time you release your breath, release the tensions right along with it. Name each area and as you release the tension from that area, say to yourself:

My (body part) is feeling very relaxed.

When you are relaxed, slowly open your eyes.

Before you do the first exercise, date the page in your journal. You need date only the first page of each day's entry.

Now, you are ready to begin.

Treasure the chaos out of which order emerges
Cherish the puzzlement leading to the light
Deep inside this nest is the self to be found

Be patient toward all that is unsolved in your heart and try to love the *questions themselves* like locked rooms and like books that are written in a very foreign tongue. . .And the point is, to live everything. *Live* the questions now. Perhaps you will then gradually, without noticing it, live along some distant day into the answer.

— Ranier Maria Rilke

Plate 10

—Albert Einstein

". . . What is in me is stronger than I am."

—Albert Camus

"Be a light unto yourself."

—Buddha's last utterance

2   Where You're At, Where You're Coming From

As the chapter title suggests, the first group of exercises focuses on your present and past. You start by exploring feelings in the immediate present and then step back for a panoramic view of your entire life up to now. You'll take inventory of *what is* and consider some changes toward *what could be.*

The purpose of these exercises is to help you:

- relax and tune into yourself
- explore and discharge feelings by drawing and writing them out
- gain insight into what's really going on inside you
- learn to clarify and express feelings more easily
- put your present into perspective by seeing it in the context of your past
- learn what your life history has to teach you
- decide what changes you want to make in the immediate future
- take action and implement changes

Take some colors and make some marks on your journal page. Try "messing around." Don't attempt to make "Art" or to draw a "picture" or plan any particular design. Don't think or pre-conceive what it will look like. Just let it happen. Let whatever wants to come out appear on the paper. Play with the colors. Find out what kinds of lines, shapes, textures, shades of color you can make. Do this as long as you like.

Uses: Especially helpful if you feel nervous about drawing, afraid you "can't draw" or will make "ugly art." It's also useful as a relaxation technique if you are tense or tired. You can turn your head off and just fool around without any goal in mind.

This is a good way to loosen up and get started, the way dancers limber up their bodies or musicians tune up their instruments. These drawing and writing tools are your instruments and you need to know them and what you can do with them.

Plate 11A

Plate 11 B

HOW DO I FEEL RIGHT NOW?

Turn your attention inward and ask yourself:

How do I feel right now?

Close your eyes and meditate on the question for awhile. Pay attention to physical sensations and emotional feelings. See if any visual images or words come to mind which express how you feel at this moment in time.

_____

While your eyes were closed, you may have seen images, colors, words, or symbols. Or you simply may have felt some physical sensations or emotions. Channel them out in any form or style: doodles, scribbles, shapes, textures, images, or words.

_____

When you are finished, look over what you have done. Do you have any reactions? If so, write them down on the next page in your journal.

_____

Uses: This is perhaps the basic and most often-used exercise in Creative Journal-keeping. It is especially helpful when you have very powerful feelings that are difficult to handle. You can pinpoint exactly how you feel and then examine and clarify what you want to do with your feelings in everyday life. This exercise encourages you to pause and reflect, to discharge or release feelings, to sort out and clarify and, perhaps, articulate more clearly where you're at.

A scribble becomes graffiti

Plate 12

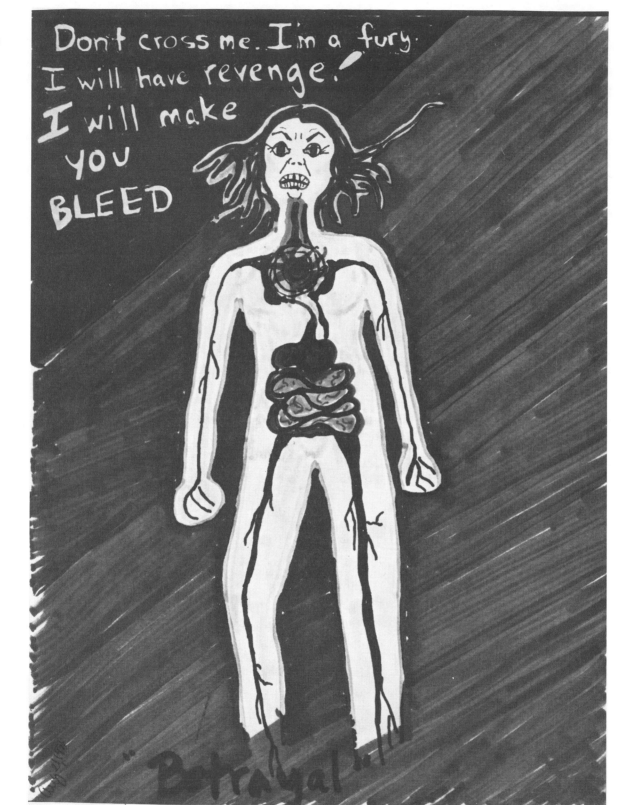

24

Plate 13

Poetry is rhyming—control—the feelings come out in iambic penta-meter. But sometimes the metre costs a feeling. I will write what spills out onto the page from my crowded life. A pause—I wonder now, what about education, career, children, marriage and the fami-ly. How can a "romantic" become mechanized to the rhythm of so many external needs and also pursue my own. I feel old—tired and grey. Fulfilling goals—to what end? A goal only evaporates anyway. I can't even find my sense of humor. Life seems so tedious and con-stricted. I feel so tired of trying. Maybe that's the key. Stop trying. But then life would be a void. So there's the polarity—the crowded construction or the void. I wonder—those people in cars—driving with pinched faces and frowns. Have they lost their will to smile? Have they had the same difficulty finding a peaceful "middle" ground? The books give labels to my feelings—anxiety, depression, regression. But labels are only tags and they change with the "price of tea." I don't like tags. Optimism. Good word. Tomorrow will be different. Nice philosophy. Poor Don Quixote. He must have felt ridiculous—batting away at those windmills. And even Sancho Panza got weary.

And the tears won't come and the smile won't break and a feeling of heaviness surrounds my shoulders. I should think I would feel guilty indulging in all this self pity—if I could even feel self pity. I suppose the most prominent feeling is impotence and purposelessness. I know this sounds morbid as hell. But that's how I feel and I'm tired of pretending. And maybe by allowing myself these black feelings, I will be more receptive to the brighter ones, and accept this cloudy day without excuses and apologies.

Plate 14

26   depression

hovers and hangs
over me like a
living thing.
it swallows me
it starts at my
edges and takes
small bites—
then keeps eating
away in my
head—till i
am no more.
i am consumed
by this thing.
i want to fight back
but
i let it take me—
it's so easy to be
eaten alive—
bit by bit
by words
by anger
by resentment
till there is

nothing

Plate 15

How can I speak my joy in words?
I can't remain within the boundaries of nouns
and verbs ... so I flow into the poetry of
words and pictures, of song and sound,
of movement ... the singing of my body
the gestures of my soul.
Hold me earth and sea,
take me up wind and clouds.
Hold me in your arms –
I am floating away.

PEACE IS ALIVE IN ME TAKING ME HIGHER THAN I EVER DREAMED

Plate 16

MY INNER AND OUTER SELF

Ask yourself the question:

What do my inner and outer self look and feel like at this time in my life?

Think of your *inner self* as your internal, private world of physical sensations, emotional feelings, fantasies, memories, wishes, thoughts. Your *outer self* is the part of you that shows to the outside world, the ways in which you express yourself for others to see: your activities, behavior, accomplishments, body, environment. Close your eyes and meditate on your inner and outer self.

———————————————————————

Some images may have come to you which reflect the quality of your inner and outer self at this time. They may be contrasting. For instance, you may feel very active inside with many thoughts and feelings buzzing around. Your external world, on the other hand, might seem quiet, calm or even boring and stagnant.

Draw an expression of your inner and outer self. Use any style that feels right for you: doodles, images, symbols, pictures. You may express both your inner and outer self in one drawing or you may want to use two separate pages if that is more appropriate for you.

———————————————————————

Afterwards, look at what you drew. On your next journal page, write your impressions, thoughts, feelings about what your graphic expression "says" to you.

———————————————————————

Uses: This is a tool for examining conflict and gaining perspective.

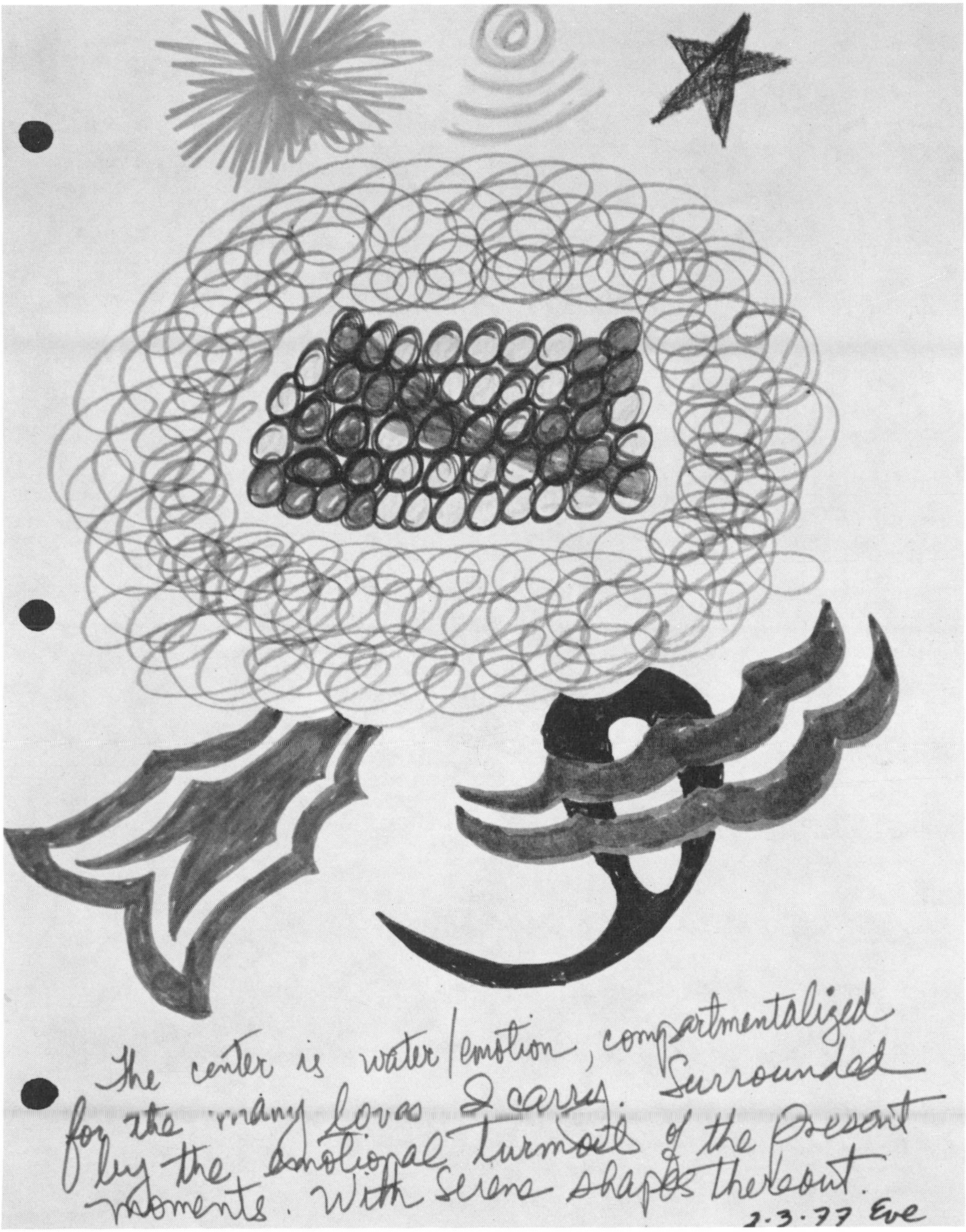

The center is water/emotion, compartmentalized
for the many loves I carry. Surrounded
by the emotional turmoil of the present
moments. With serene shapes thereabout.

2·3·77 Eve

Plate 17

I feel like the external world is creeping in on my private space. It feels like a wave is just about to crest then come crashing down on me.

If I can muster the energy I'm going to push back the wave and run home free from the power and force of the whole mess.

The energy pushing on me is so powerful. The counterforce to bring to bear is tremendous.

Plate 18 A

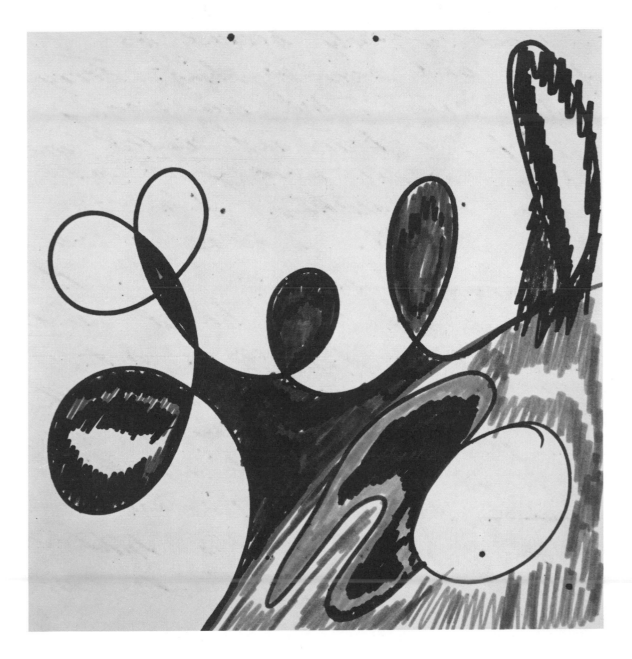

Plate 18B

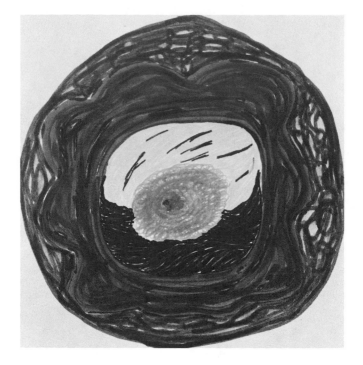

My Center

I need
to
protect
you,
my center

But
I don't
want
to
encase
you
in
a hard shell
so that
you
aren't
available
for me

Plate 19 A

So,
I need
to
have
you
available
to me
but
also —
safe

How do
I
do
that?

Keep
the layers
connected!
Keep
in touch
with the center
layers —
Encase the vulnerable center with Wisdom!
She will help you.

Two "inner/outer self" drawings done by the same woman 17 days apart. The second one, shown above, suggests that there's been an opening up and expansion.

Plate 19 B

LOOKING BACK

Look back over the day and ask yourself:

What kind of day was it? What were the highlights?

Close your eyes and, in your mind's eye, replay the movie of your day. Start out by visualizing the first waking moment and then go on to retrace your steps through the day up to the present moment. Recall what happened as best you can, pausing for a second at the highlights: the significant thoughts, feelings, events, interactions, people, places.

Draw or write about the highlights of the day. About each one, ask:

How did I feel at the time? How do I feel about it now?

Afterward, study over what you have drawn or written and add any comments.

Variations: This exercise can be used to focus on longer periods of time, such as a week, month, year, or whatever block of time has meaning for you.

Uses: At the end of the day (or any other period of time), this exercise can help you tie up loose ends, clear your mind, put things into perspective and perhaps clarify some lines of future action.

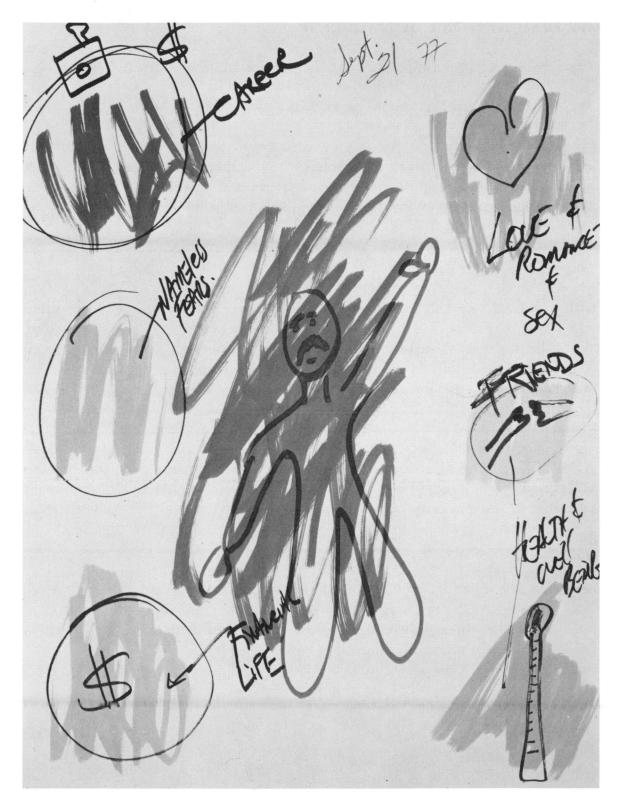

Day in Review:

Plate 20

MY LIFE HISTORY: A TIME LINE

Think back over your entire life up to the present and ask yourself:

What have been the key events and experiences in my life?

Go back to your very first memories and go slowly through your life. Close your eyes as you do this in order to more clearly visualize your memories. Pause to reflect upon the most significant events and periods of time. Recall the experiences and feelings associated with them as vividly as you can.

Draw a time line as shown in plate 21. Fill in key years on the "yard-stick," starting with your birth year and ending with the current year. To the right of the time line, write in a word or phrase for each key event or experience. Directly across, to the left of the time line, write in the feelings (physical, emotional) you had at the time or during that period in your life. You may want to color in each period of the "yardstick", using a color that expresses how you were feeling then.

When you are finished, study your life history time line. Write or draw the thoughts or feelings you have about any part or all of your life as you view it in retrospect. Take note of any patterns, cycles, themes, lessons that you see revealed there.

Uses: This time line is an invaluable tool or map for further explorations of the self through such forms as autobiographical writings, short stories, poems, drawings of scenes, events, people. It is also helpful for doing self-inventory of repeated patterns and cycles.

MY LIFE HISTORY: A TIME LINE

The key events go above the line,
your feelings and reactions at the time go below the line.

Feelings (below)	Year	Key events (above)
	1937	
very happy, secure, felt loved but sometimes lonely as only child.	40	—moved to new neighborhood
very happy, creative	41	—went to kindergarten
hated school, felt like a prison	42	—started grammar school, 1st grade
much happier, loved music, got praise and encouragement for talent. Still hated school, except for English & choir.	44	—started piano lessons
	47	—very ill with pneumonia, started drawing while recovering
happy, "in love" with painting	50	—started classes at art school on Sat.
miserable 1st two yrs. high school. Difficulty adjusting to moving, adolescence.	51	—started high school moved to new neighborhood, new school
	77	

Plate 21

My parents were lonely and insecure. Because they didn't have much money they envied those that did and regarded them as snobs. However, my parents were really snobs. They were very prejudiced regarding other religions and races (than ours) with the exception of the Italians. When we first came to L.A.—my parent's first real friends were the Fiore's—they are still friends. However, they thought the Fiore's a bit eccentric—with all that "sanctimonious" church-going and lavish Xmas dinners. Actually my parents loved those dinners—but envied the family because they were wealthy. They often commented on their frivolous expenditures on jewelry and mink coats. They also felt that their 3 children were just terrific, especially the eldest. But what a shame they were so spoiled.

I used to get hand-me-down clothes (my first cashmere sweater). I hated it. My mother made my clothes—using the "finest fabrics" (from the Home Silk Shop), hopefully bargain remnants. My mother was a terrific seamstress (a fact that is ingrained in my head)—a perfectionist! She insisted that I try on the particular garment-in-progress at least 2 dozen times. As I mentioned, my mother was a perfectionist—but so was I. So it was—we discussed, lamented and argued endlessly about the length of the hem, the width of the skirt, the size of the buttonholes, the color of the buttons and the "fit" of the garment. (This was the most brutal part.) We would never agree. The result was a nicely home-made dress, which was perfectly tailored, according to my mother's standards—and embarrassingly "gross" according to my standards. When my mother bought me a store-bought garment, the first requirement was that it had to be a bargain. And if we couldn't readily find a bargain, my mother would drag me from store to store examining price tags and seams until the purchase of the dress was not worth the exhaustion and guilt (because she rarely failed to mention that she could have done a far better job at a lesser cost.) So I would wear my new-old twice-marked-down Lanz dress, Alas! I should have felt like a princess. Instead, I felt like Cinderella's Step-sister (no matter how many compliments I would get).

Plate 22A

Ready for the big night—pictures were taken— a lengthy process because of my tendency to frown (my mother was constantly admonishing that great lines would soon appear between my eyebrows if I did not stop frowning) so now I use tons of moisturizer! My husband is hard-put to understand this phobia—much less the expense. And so were the rudiments of a lousy self-image.

My one saving grace. I looked like a "shiksa"—a fact that my parents would constantly reinforce. All their neighbors and friends commented on my light hair, blue eyes and "pug" nose. Another incongruity. I was to be proud of being Jewish and at the same time looking like a "shiksa." And my main goal in life was to look like Audrey Hepburn. (Well, we had the same flat chest.)

I also made mad love to my pillow trying to actualize James Dean or Rock Hudson. In reality I did not make mad love because my parents told me that nice girls didn't do that sort of thing. So I fell in love with the toughest "rogue" in junior high, Rick Carter—a combination of James Dean and Rock Hudson. He liked me because I was a "nice" girl. We talked in the hall. We talked in class. And I drew pictures of Rick kissing me with great passion. He never kissed me. He just kept telling me how much he liked me because I was such a pretty—nice—girl. Someday, he said, someone would "deserve" me. My parents told me that, too. And so I waited for someone to "deserve" me and was "honored" in the school Slam Book as the class prude. My God, what a terrific honor! My parents were proud.

And so it was—I became untouchable—the all-American-girl who fantasized being a passionate femme fatale. A pretty young girl who doubted her physical assets, fading into a world of dreams because reality seemed so ambiguous— and much of the time very lonely (I'm an only child) and painful—I heard my parents fighting at night. I thought that I wanted to die because we didn't live like Ozzie and Harriet.

Reflections on the above

After re-reading the above I am amused at the feelings bubbling from the past. I felt very sad when reading the end. My reactions up until now were feelings of sorrow relating to my childhood family life. I now feel that the tears were really meant for the present; that my own present life is not a T.V. fantasy, picket fence and roses. It's not Ozzie and Harriet floating through sunny days, solving problems with ease and grace. It's just not that simple. It's damn hard work!

Plate 22B

WHERE AM I AT?

Reflect upon this period in your life and ask yourself:

Where am I at in my life right now?

Think about what kind of a time this is for you. See if there was a particular event or experience that marked the beginning of this period. Then think about the chief characteristics of this period, the quality of your life right now. Is it a hectic time? A calm period? A time of crisis? A period of transition and change? A dull, stagnant period? Close your eyes and meditate on your life at the present time.

_____

Draw any images, colors, forms that reflect where you are at in your life at this particular time. Also, write about this period.

_____

Uses: This is an excellent way to take stock periodically, to keep current with your inner response to the conditions that surround you. This gives you a chance to see what is happening and opens up options for change if that feels appropriate. It can be a way to appreciate what your life is like and enjoy it even more if this is a good time for you.

Changing
Currents

Plate 23

To get out of the pit
I can stand up. To do
that would put part of me
in the light. There can be a
sequence of events or choices
thereafter:

Crawl the rest of the
way out into the light
or
retreat back into the black hole

Which is it going
to be Robin?

Plate 24 A

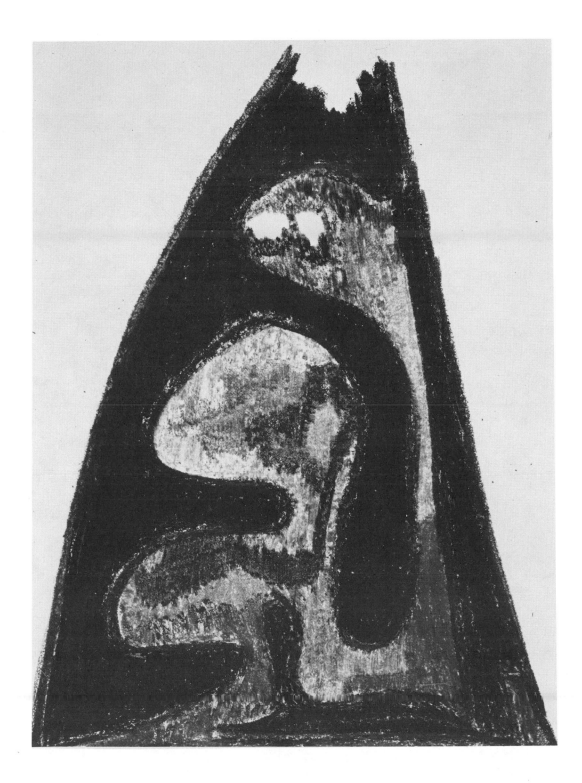

Plate 24 B

44

Journal –
    This is ridiculous. I'm going through another cycle of heartaches. I thought I was all over Bill but that empty feeling keeps returning. It's like a lump in my throat only the lump got lost and is in my heart. Once school gets going I'll be fine but for the time being I hurt.
    It's so strange – I love him but I know it'd never work again cause of my weird moods.
    I miss Chris to but that's another lost feeling of the heart. That's like a whole in my heart.
    I just want to cry. I'm so crabby. I want to kill coina, elevate Bill, and Befriend Chris H. Well whatever God gives me is right so may my heart be open.

Plate 25

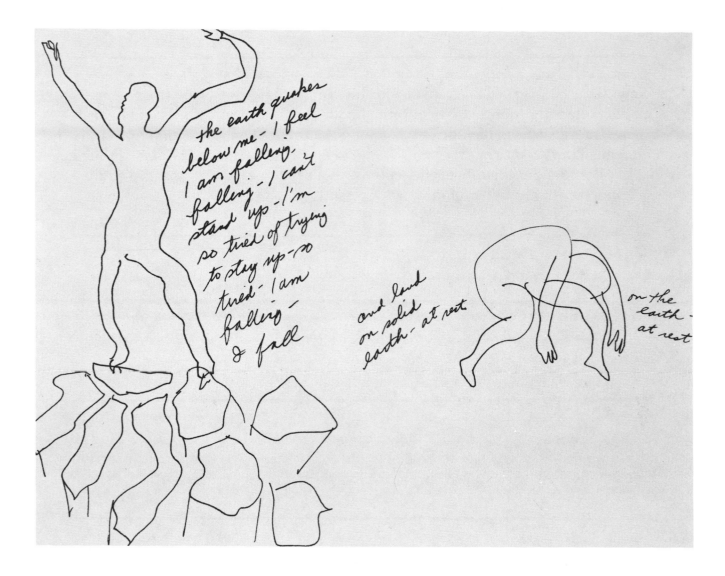

the earth quakes below me — I feel I am falling, falling — I can't stand up — I'm so tired of trying to stay up — so tired — I am falling — I fall

and land on solid earth — at rest

on the earth — at rest

Coping with crisis — Plate 26

TIME/LIFE MAP

Imagine your typical week (or day or month). Think about all the activities and functions you perform, the roles you play, responsibilities you have, the things you like to do. Visualize yourself in all these aspects of your life. Be aware of how much time and importance you give to each one.

Now, make a "map" or diagram of your life. Draw a large shape on the page, e.g., circle, rectangle, square, or free form. Divide the shape up into sections which represent the aspects of your life that you visualized. Let each section reflect the amount of importance or time that you give to that aspect. This can be done through size, color, design. Identify each section with a symbol, color, or image. You may label each with a word or phrase, if you wish.

Study your map and ask yourself:

> *Are there any aspects of my life that I want to change? Are there some I'd like to limit or drop altogether? Are there some things missing which I want to include in my life?*

Make a new map of a week (day, month), but as you would like it to be, including in it all the things you'd like to be doing and experiencing. Again, let each section reflect the importance you *really* place on the aspect, activity, role, etc.

Examine the changes you put into your new map. Think about how you will implement these changes in the coming week or month. Write your observations and intentions on the next page in your journal. Check back in a week or so to see how you are doing.

Variations: Focus on only *one* area of your life: work schedule, leisure time activities, diet and eating pattern, exercise. Do a map of it.

Uses: This map shows how you set your priorities and demonstrates that you create your life values and use of time, whether by conscious choice or by default. It's still up to you to decide.

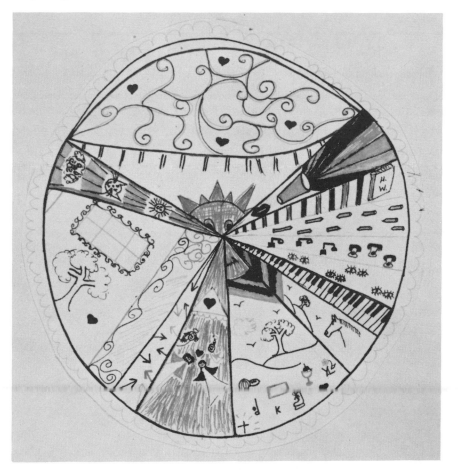

Picture Time/Life Map   Plate 27

DO LIKE AND DON'T LIKE

Think about the present time in your life and ask:

> *What do I like about myself and my life right now?*

Visualize yourself in the aspects of your personality, in the settings and situations you like so much. Include such things as behavior, attitudes, physical characteristics, skills, and achievements. Picture the environments, activities, relationships you enjoy most. Experience the good feelings associated with all these elements.

Head your journal page: *Do Like* . . . and underneath that, list all those things you like about yourself and your life at the present time.

Study the list over. Is there anything you have forgotten? Is there something new you'd like to add to improve yourself or enhance your life in some way? Is there anything you'd like to expand or strengthen? Write these items down in a second list (perhaps in a different color). Now, write a contract with yourself to add at least one new *Do Like* element to your life in the coming week. Write out how you will actually do this and check in a week to see how you are doing. (Use a longer time span if necessary.)

Now ask yourself:

> *What don't I like about myself and my life right now?*

As you think about this question, be as honest with yourself as possible.

On a new journal page, make a heading that reads: *Don't like* . . . Then list all the things you don't like about yourself and your life right now.

Study the list of *Don't Likes* carefully. Choose one item to focus on during the coming week. Underline the item and then write out a brief contract with yourself agreeing to observe this particular aspect of yourself or your life during the coming week. Then agree to deal with it in some way. You might decide to change it or accept it as is for now. If you decide to change, then write down your ideas and plans for putting the change into effect. Check at the week's end to see how you did. (If it is a change that will take longer, give yourself whatever time is practical for implementing it.)

Uses: This provides an excellent opportunity to inventory yourself and take control of your life in very specific and concrete ways. By focussing on one item, one week at a time, you give yourself a chance to succeed in changing elements that have nagged you for a long time. Sometimes, items from the *Don't Like* list will vanish, as if by magic, without much effort. Perhaps by simply recognizing them, we release them.

As with the previous exercise, this inventory enables you to make more conscious choices instead of being swept along by external circumstances and events.

THE KEY WORD

Ask yourself the question:

> *What is the theme of my personal growth at this particular time? What word describes the current challenge or lesson I'm dealing with right now?*

Write down the key word or phrase at the top of your journal page. Then make a list of words that pop into your mind in connection with this word or phrase. Don't *think* about it. Just let the words flow out quickly and spontaneously in free-association. Let one word trigger the next in a chain reaction.

Read over your word chain and write down any reactions or comments.

Uses: When a particular theme or issue keeps recurring in your experience this is a means to explore its significance for you. Also, if a particular word evokes a strong physical reaction, it's worth examining.

J. asked me to marry him. The word "marriage" hit me. I had such a strong gut reaction I decided to explore it.

Free-Association/Marriage

Need
Dependence
Freedom
Imprisonment
Inter-dependence
Inter-twining
Loss of Self-hood
Union
The One and the Many
Coming Together
Joining
Separating
Breaking apart
Fear
Abandonment
Enrichment
Cooperation
Individuation
Loss of self
Merging
Paradox
Giving Up
Giving

Strength
Weakness
Bond
Vow
Promise
Commitment
Communication
Interaction
Meeting
Creating
Greeting
Protecting
Bordering
Holding
Releasing
Binding
Gentleness
Tenderness
Support
Comfort
Cherish
Respect
Love

Passion
Patience
Separateness
Growth
Questioning
Feeling
Sensing
Telling
Listening
Compassion
Empathy
Companionship
Struggle
Work
Pain
Sadness
Family
Estrangement
Isolation
Loneliness
Misunderstanding
Ending
Beginning

Nesting
Living Together
Building
Ritual
Contract
Broken
Divorce
Grieving
Resurrection
Courage
Thoughtfulness
Affection
Shyness
Touching
Closeness
Intimacy
Sharing
Giving
Liking
Mutuality
Reciprocal
Equality
Balance

In Love
Embracing
Making Love
Merging
Blending
Consolation
Caring
Understanding
Foundation
Peace
Being Loved
Loving
Acceptance
Detachment
Involvement
Faithfulness
Consciousness
Trust
Confidence
Risk
Vulnerability
Nurturing
Helping
Gather together
In Common

51

Plate 28

CURRENT CHALLENGE

Think about the major challenge or problem in your life right now. Ask yourself:

What am I struggling with? Is it within me or without?

Close your eyes and visualize your struggle. See if any images come to mind. Really feel the nature of the struggle and see if you have any physical reactions or symptoms that seem related to it, e.g., "pain in the neck", headache, upset stomach, etc.

Draw the struggle. Give the drawing a name.

Let the drawing speak to you. Imagine what it would say to you if it could talk. Respond to it and write out your conversation on another page as though it were a script for a play.

Uses: When you are especially plagued with worry, tension, etc., this exercise can help you get to the heart of the problem and lead the way to confronting the problem and resolving it. If you uncover physical symptoms in connection with this exercise, turn to *My Body, My Self* as a continuation (Pg. 112). It deals directly with physical reactions and their causes and possible preventive measures.

"Final Examinations: Tension & Anxiety"   Plate 29

Plate 30

"Nothing is more sacred than the laws of our own nature and we must thoroughly look within ourselves and not permit outside standards to be imposed upon us."

—Ralph Waldo Emerson

"The universe resounds with the joyful cry, I am."

—Scriabin

3   Who You Are

Here is a mirror for examining your self-image and identity. In these excercises, you'll come face to face with feelings and beliefs that form the very foundation of who you are and how you experience life. You'll explore the many facets and dimensions of your personality and private inner reality. This includes taking inventory, assessing inner resources, and identifying changes you want to make. After focussing on the diverse aspects of yourself, you'll then put it all together to realize the whole person that you are.

These exercises are intended to help you:

- see yourself more clearly
- see the relationship between self-concept and quality of life experience
- explore your roles, functions, "public image"
- recognize and affirm your personal resources and strengths
- assess abilities and discover new interests
- uncover buried talent and potential
- identify and visualize desired changes
- study the variety of aspects or many selves which you contain
- integrate your many aspects into a you-nified whole person

Close your eyes and do the relaxation exercise (Pg. 16). With eyes still closed, turn your attention inward and be with yourself quietly for awhile. Experience simply *being you*. Then ask yourself:

How do I see myself?

Focus on your perception of yourself using your inner eye. See if some visual images come to mind in the form of symbols, colors, shapes. Or you may experience thoughts or feelings or visualize your physical appearance as you imagine it, see it in mirrors or photographs.

_____

Let your perception of yourself flow out onto your journal page in some form of drawn expression.

_____

Study the drawing over and see what it "says" to you. Write down your feelings and thoughts in response to what you see on the page.

_____

With your eyes closed, focus inward again. This time ask yourself:

How would I like *to see myself?*

Now draw an image of how you would like to perceive yourself, a projection of the person you want to become.

_____

Let your drawing speak, introducing itself in the first person. Let it tell about itself and then write down what it says.

_____

Uses: This exercise reveals your present self-image and your self-concept in general. You can examine how your perception and beliefs about yourself affect your attitudes, behavior, and expectations. You can also see how you create limitations for yourself and pin-point areas in need of change.

Through positive auto-suggestion in the form of visualization of your desired self-image, you can learn to build up the attitudes and beliefs necessary to bring about satisfying changes. This is an excellent example of applied creativity in everyday life. By using your imagination and creative expression to project a new you, you are affirming your strength and directing your life toward greater fulfillment.

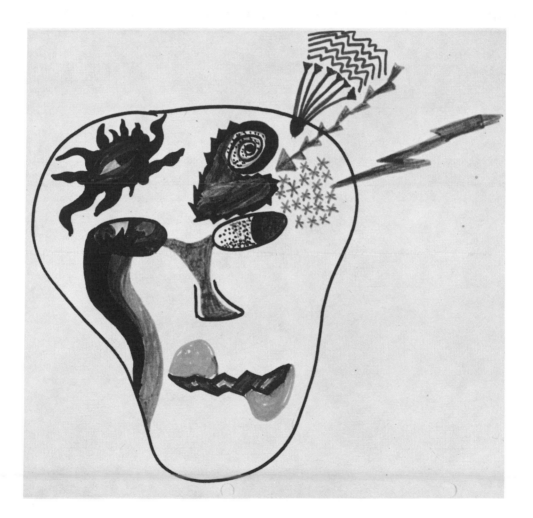

Plate 31

Plate 32 A

Self-portrait

My Self-Portrait drawing is symbolically in boxes and the box inside a box inside a box. The different colors represent my layers of personality, green, the protective outside color that holds me together, purple, the personality of passion, the orange represents knowledge and the center core of yellow is the core of light at my center using knowledge to protect it. The light beams penetrate to the other layers of my personality trying to penetrate through the other colors of blue which is part of my depressive nature. It is significant to me that whenever I describe my self today I feel in boxes, or that these feelings keep me boxed in. I also see the rigidity I place on myself.

Plate 32 B

IN SILENT SOLITUDE
I FLOAT OUT
FLOWING
IN SLOWEST
MOTION
SERENE
DAUGHTER
OF MY
DEEPEST
SELF

Plate 33

I listened to the secret silent voice within
She spoke softly, singing to herself in the night.
She cried inside me
She dreamed and whispered
I listened
She screamed to be heard,
to be free to see the sun
to touch the moon.

I held her, crooning a mother's hymn
held her
my daughter, my joy
my self
held her
glowing
within
me

Epiphany
January 6 · 1974

Plate 34

In this drawing I feel this woman, (me) is at a standstill emerging from her cocoon of a leaf of growth. Her throat is marked—thwarting her voice, my voice. Her arms are bound behind her, restricting her getting out of the cocoon or at least not helping. I feel that in my growth now my hands are tied by circumstance. Her expression is not a happy one but sad, longing, questionable look. A perplexing look, a look I know too well. This growth that is at a halt is interesting because it is I that is holding back myself. Afraid to go on, afraid to break the barriers.

Plate 35A

It felt very good to draw the woman in the first picture again (here) *as I would like to see her.* I made her open: showing the beauty she's held, I've held, wrapped up around me. Her hair flowing and beautiful as wings of a butterfly. Her arms strong with movement and freedom. Her legs dancing gently on a huge leaf of growth. Her face is pleased with herself—body and soul. This is me to be, a place to come to when I've explored my past away to expose the beauty there is now—how nice to be free from the old chains that I had placed on me! How nice!!!

Plate 35 B

WHAT'S IN A NAME

Go back in your memory as far back as you can. Remember all the names you have been called. Start with the name on your birth certificate. Make a list of all your names in chronological order, including nick-names, names taken in marriage, titles that went before or after your name.

Read the list of names over and write down any reactions you have.

On another page, make a graphic design built upon the letters of your name. Use any part or all of your current name if you wish, e.g., initials, first name or last name only, etc. As you form the letters, let them evolve into an expression of who you are. Integrate any other images, symbols, shapes to create your own "illuminated manuscript" or personal logo design.

Write down your reactions to your name design.

Write a poem about your name or a word-play using the name itself, e.g., rhyming, syllables repeated.

Uses: Here you can explore the relationship between your name, your roles, and image to the outside world. You can see the significance of your name as an expression of your personality and your life history. You can also examine the deeper meaning and personal symbolism of your name as one aspect of your identity.

A Name Story design   Plate 36

LOGO:

It is simple, complete, unadorned with frou-frou. It reminds me of a window; sectioned horizontally in the middle, suggesting more than one part, but equal parts. It is open and visibility is possible from the inside and the outside. It is a satisfying symbol of how I feel.

Surprisingly, 4 letters are incorporated; O, E, A, B. The "O" I dropped years ago, the B is not of my choice. (I've been thinking of dropping my "married" name). But the true logo seemed to need all four of the initials to be complete; therefore this logo drawing and it's O.K. now.

Write a letter to an unknown person. Introduce yourself and tell who you are. Describe your appearance, background, activities, interests, and concerns. You might include something about where you live, work, or go to school (the environments you spend your time in) as well as the significant people in your life.

Read the letter back to yourself, imagining you are the stranger who has received the letter. Write down your reactions to the letter.

Focus your attention inward with closed eyes. Meditate on the phrase: "I am. . ." completing it many times in your imagination. Then, write a poem entitled, *I Am . . .* Don't worry about rhyming or structure, just let it flow in free verse. You may want to illustrate the poem as well.

Uses: This exercise provides an opportunity to step back and view yourself and your context (personal history, environment, people, etc.) It gives you another perspective for viewing the totality of who you are. It also suggests a new vehicle for communication through poetry.

I am a woman
who once chose to bear grief
who then chose to bury grief
who then walked from burial grounds
To the sea.
I am a woman who chooses
To risk the tide
To be trusted by waves
To swim, float, sail. . .
I am a woman who chooses.

Plate 38

We have never spoken but I have seen you from time to
time and know you would be a good and understanding friend.
I'm writing to you today to tell you about myself.
I've been working very hard the last two years to change
my life style, to free myself from old habits and beliefs
that no longer are valid. Sometimes in those two
years I wondered how crazy it was to work so hard
for change when it seemed safer to remain invisible and
ineffective. It's only by looking back at those days
that I get a good feeling about now. I am making my
own decisions now and taking responsibility for them. I feel good
about that. I still get angry with myself when I fall back
into passive ways because I'm afraid. My mind knows there's
nothing to fear but fear itself, but my gut is frequently
gutless.

I'm very good at working and persevering but what I really
want is for you to come out of the mist and hold me and tell me
I'm O.K. I tell myself I'm O.K., but not often enough and often
I don't believe myself. I'm very lonely and incomplete without
you. It's easy for me to love and care for others but
not easy for me to love and care for myself.

> I am the glimmering trail
> of a fallen tear
> I am the silence
> of longing

Plate 39

Close your eyes and ask yourself:

>   *What do I believe about myself? What are my personality traits? My patterns of behavior? My talents and potential? My limitations?*

Meditate upon these questions for awhile.

Divide the page vertically down the middle into two columns. Head the left column: *Beliefs about myself.* Head the right hand column: *Where they came from.* Now, write down the beliefs you hold about yourself in the left column. Include positive and negative beliefs.

Review your list of beliefs about yourself. As you read each one, ask:

>   *Where did this belief come from? Have others told me this about myself? Have I developed this belief on my own?*

In the right hand column, across from each belief statement, write down the names of people who have told you this about yourself. If you can't remember hearing it from anyone else, then leave it blank or fill in your own name.

Re-read the list of beliefs and where they came from. Put a check by the beliefs that you *don't* like. Examine where they came from and ask yourself if you want to change these beliefs about yourself. If so, turn to a new page in your journal and rewrite each belief that you wish to change. Rewrite the belief in a positive form *as if* you'd already changed your attitude and behavior or situation.

Example: *Old belief*   *New belief*
                I am a clumsy person.   I am a graceful person.

Do this with as many beliefs as you wish to change.

Meditate on each new belief, visualizing yourself in everyday life manifesting the desired quality or behavior, *as if* you'd already achieved the state of being you wish to possess. Then relax and have faith that "what you set your heart on will surely be yours," to quote Emerson.

Uses: This exercise is designed to help you build a positive self-image and change negative patterns of belief and behavior. By getting to the roots of negative beliefs, you can start weeding them out of your life one by one. This exercise can help you take control of your life by helping you strengthen your foundation: the personal belief system which holds you up (if it's positive) or lets you down (if it's negative). You can see how limitation was programmed into your mind and start disentangling yourself from such destructive thought patterns. You have the power to drop negativity and to reprogram positive messages into your personal belief system. The results will not be immediate, but if you are patient and learn to have faith in the power of your imagination, your behavior and expectations will be affected in a positive way. Your beliefs about yourself color everything you take in from the world around you and the way you project yourself out into the world.

Close your eyes and ask yourself:

> *What are my beliefs about life in general? What is my philosophy of life at the present time?*

Meditate upon this. Give yourself plenty of time to think about it.

Write down your beliefs, your own philosophy of life based on your experiences.

Afterward, read it over. Then compare it with your beliefs about yourself from Part One of the exercise. See what observations you make. Write them down, if you wish.

Uses: This exercise is intended to help you delve deeper into your belief system. It can highlight any conflicts in your beliefs which may be creating an impasse or stalemate situation. For instance, one female student shared that she had been raised to believe that successful career women were hard, unfeminine, lonely creatures (old belief), yet she was talented, had a desire and the financial need to pursue a career along with a new belief that this is a valuable direction for her personal growth. She has encouragement to enter a career from her women friends and from the women's movement. Yet, her old beliefs about the lonely career woman are still haunting her, putting her career goals constantly into question, raising doubts, feeding her lack of self-confidence and fear of failure. She is in a double-bind; fear of success and fear of failure. She will need to deal with this dilemma before she can proceed.

SELF-INVENTORY

Think about all the things you've accomplished which give you pride in yourself. Ask yourself:

What skills and talents do I possess? What areas of knowledge have I gained? What are my positive personality traits and qualities? What have been my most important achievements, the ones of which I am most proud?

Make four lists and head them:

1. My skills and talents
2. My areas of knowledge and experience
3. My positive personality traits and qualities
4. My most important achievements

Then fill in each list.

Read the self-inventory lists over and write down any feelings or thoughts you have in reaction.

Uses: This is a tool for assessing your inner resources. It is especially effective when you are embarking on a new venture, starting a new career, changing jobs, in the midst of major life transitions. It is highly useful for building self-confidence and affirming your own worth during periods of self-doubting and insecurity, a way to "keep the faith" in yourself.

Close your eyes and ask yourself:

> *What does the word* creative *mean to me personally? How does the creative spirit live in me? How do I express my creativity in my everyday life, activities, relationships?*

Meditate upon your *creative self.*

Draw your creative self in any graphic style that feels right for you: symbols, abstract design, doodles, cartoon, picture, etc.

Look at what you've drawn and write down your reactions. Then let your creative self speak to you (in the first person, singular), e.g. "I am your creative self . . ." and write it out in your journal. Have a conversation with your creative self, if you wish, asking questions and responding to what it says to you.

Uses: This exercise can help you explore and expand your definition of creativity and to actively experience and express this innate human characteristic. By recognizing and cherishing the creativity you already use without perhaps being consciously aware of it, you can tap hidden potential. This exercise helps you to affirm yourself as you are now and to build inner strength and self-esteem for taking on new challenges.

Plate 40

Plate 41

A Tree —

A lot of prior talk about roots in the name exercise suggested a tree. At first my mind went blank — I looked at the blank page & knew that my creative self is bound up with blank pages that I must fill if I am to be a writer. Symbolically, the blank page was the image I had. Then I drew a tree with large deep roots and many branches because I also know that what I write will be about myself and all that has gone into me & come from me — the roots and the branches. The foliage on the tree is rich and healthy — it is not a bare tree. It is nourished and nourishing and good to see.

PARTS OF MYSELF

Close your eyes and say to yourself:

I contain within myself many qualities or aspects. What are they?

Meditate upon your personality traits and characteristics.

Create a graphic design in which you represent the different parts or aspects of yourself, the many qualities you possess, such as: feelings, intellect, humor, sexuality, etc. Find the labels that best describe your own unique qualities. You may want to write these labels into the design.

Look at the finished design and write down your reactions.

Select one of the parts or aspects you portrayed. On another page, draw a more detailed picture of it. Then let the drawing speak to you (first person) and write down what it says. Also let it speak to other parts in your original drawing. Or you can simply let parts of the drawing speak to each other in a written conversation.

Uses: This is an opportunity to discover the many facets of your personality and how each element relates to the others. You may uncover some conflict which is creating stress and dividing the self. Through dialogs with the parts, you can work toward some resolution and integration, developing a sense of unity within. Of course, this is a continual process of inner balancing and never ends at a fixed point of arrival. It is ever-evolving.

Plate 42

Plate 43   Me looking at the moon: my woman-ness, my femininity

Miss Halo: I'm more acceptable to people. They don't like looking at you. I smile and do good things. I'm nice!

Ms. Red: But I smile, too and I smile to please myself, not others.

Miss Halo: Oh—do you think I'm dishonest in smiling?

Ms. Red: Yes, I do and I don't like it. Be strong! Fine, if you feel like doing "good" things, but only if you want to—not because it will make you holier than thou. Are you trying to put God out of business!?!

Miss Halo: Of course not, but people pay attention to me when I do good things. They praise me and that feels good.

Ms. Red: So you're using people to do your building of self-esteem? You're making them do your work. Sounds pretty lazy, conceited and selfish to me.

Miss Halo: Well, how dare you! How could you!?!

Ms. Red How could I? Easily. I could! You lord yourself over people and still you think you're Miss Goodness. You are worse than a dope peddler selling to children.

Miss Halo: Okay, okay so you know my game. It seems to me if what you say is true then I'm pretty smart although my ways are too self-motivated. I can say one thing, Ms. Red, you sure broke through my crusty candy coating. It feels kind of nice out here with you. Honest—honest, that's what you are!

Plate 44

Imagine yourself in the center of the blank journal page before you. Close your eyes and picture yourself located there, looking out at the world from your place in the center of the page. Then think about all the qualities you possess. Meditate upon them. Picture them in your mind's eye. After you have let these random thoughts and images pass through your mind, open your eyes.

First make a dot in the center of the page. Then draw a border around the page as a frame for your design. It can be any shape: circle, square, hexagon (six-sided figure), octagon (eight-sided).

Now, return to the center point and focus your attention there. Say:

This is my center.

Then draw an image or symbol in that central area which represents your unique inner core. Then let images, colors, shapes, and lines unfold outward, emanating from your center design. Let this evolve into a self-contained graphic expression of your many aspects integrated into wholeness.

Uses: The word *mandala* means circle in Sanskrit. The mandala, a design form which radiates out from a center, is ancient and universal, appearing in the art, architecture, dance of cultures everywhere. It is the "magic circle" and often has a ritual, religious symbolism as in the rose window of medieval churches. Here, it is intended as a drawing meditation for centering and integrating the self. In times of confusion or stress it is a way to "collect your thoughts" or "gather your wits" or "pull yourself together."

In the process of creating a mandala you can reach into deep levels of your Self. This can be done repeatedly as a part of the on-going process of integration. It is a tool for developing centeredness through outward expression in graphic art.

From the whole.
pour forth the
many new parts...
and they in turn
form a new whole...
and so goes the process.
In this cycle Love is the union,
and conflict the laser.

Plate 45

Plate 46

Plate 47

Plate 48

"The supreme happiness of life is the conviction that we are loved."

—Victor Hugo

"But before I look out . . . let me first of all gaze within myself."

—Ranier Maria Rilke

4   How You Are With Yourself

Here is a closer view of your many aspects and personality traits and how they live together inside you. Some of these exercises highlight the divided self or inner conflicts, other exercises can help you toward integration so your many selves live together within you in peace and harmony. Here you will find tools for liberating the creative energy that has been blocked by old conflicts and impasses from the past. You will also be building up your inner resources and self-esteem. There are many dialogs here, both graphic and verbal, for developing clearer lines of communication and relationships with others. "As within, so without."

These exercises are designed to help you:

- see your inner conflicts more clearly
- examine the roots of your destructive patterns
- allow the various aspects of yourself to "speak up"
- let the parts of yourself communicate openly with one another
- confront your inner demons and creative blocks
- assert yourself against self-judgement, blame, and put-downs
- build up your strength through assertion and self-care
- accept and appreciate the many parts of yourself
- be more tolerant, patient, and compassionate with the parts of your self that you don't like
- learn to love your whole self

Close your eyes and go back in your memory to childhood and adolescence. Ask yourself:

> *What were the critical, put-down messages I received as a child and teen-ager?*

Recall the words that adults, parents, teachers, and other authority figures said to you which attacked your self-esteem. What messages left you feeling inadequate, worthless, unlovable, bad, and were associated with shame and guilt? Replay those messages in your mind, just as you heard them, e.g., "You're really stupid. Can't you ever get anything right?" or "You are the messiest kid in the world. Look at that room!" or "Boy, are you awkward and clumsy. You'll never amount to anything."

Divide the page vertically down the middle. You will be writing out a dialog using your right and left hand. Start with the column that is on the same side as your dominant, writing hand. Head the column: *Put-downs*. Then write down all the put-down messages exactly as you remembered them, as though you were tran-scribing a tape (as shown in the examples below).

Now, read the put-down messages back. Allow yourself to feel your gut reaction as you hear these messages right now. Then, take your pen or pencil in your *other hand* (sub-dominant, the one you normally do not write with) and head the other column: *Answer back*. You can print or write, whichever you prefer. Then answer back to each put-down message, expressing how you feel right now at this point in time, reading these statements. Answer as though you were speaking. Use your sub-dominant hand for your answer back statement.

On a new page, using your dominant, writing hand again, express how it felt to do the right hand/left hand dialog between your critical voices from childhood and adolescence and yourself as you are today. How did it feel to hear those put-downs again? How did it feel to write with your sub-dominant hand? Were you able to really answer back? If not, what was *that* like?

Uses: This exercise can help you get to the roots of your feelings of low self-esteem and then deal with them. You can literally pull your negative self-concept out by the roots. You begin by releasing some of the righteous indignation and anger you probably felt as a child and teen-ager but did not express at the time. By answering back now, you are counteracting the destructive nature of those critical voices that live on within you like old tape recordings. You can erase those old tapes by re-recording loving and nurturing messages to yourself which build up self-esteem and creative power. (See Nurturing Myself exercise Pg. 94).

Note: This exercise usually needs to be done many times. Each negative self-concept must be dealt with. These messages have been working away at your self-esteem for years so they will not be banished overnight. However, the pay-off is tremendous. This and the next exercise are the most powerful ones I know for breaking through creative blocks.

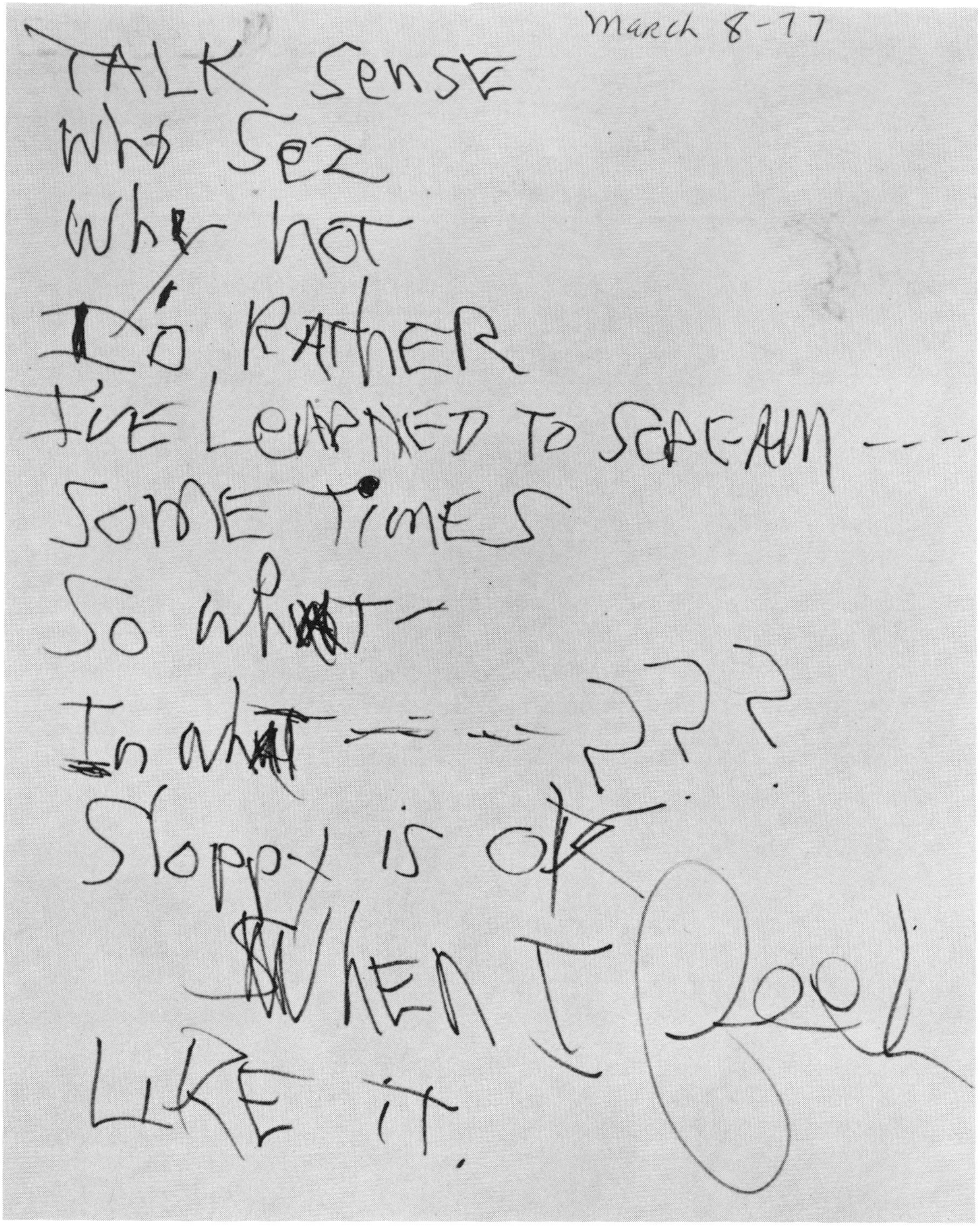

March 8-77

TALK SENSE
Who Sez
Why not
I'd RATHER
I've LEARNED TO SCREAM ----
SOME TIMES
So what -
In what --- ???
Sloppy is OK
        WHEN I feel
LIKE it.

Plate 49A

3-8-77

Speak when you're spoken too
Children should Be Seen + not heard
Don't Take chances
Don't talk to Strangers
Don't Be noisy
You're Lazy
You're A Big awkward cow
You're Sloppy

MY CRITICAL AND ASSERTIVE SELVES

Close your eyes and ask:

What are the things I say to myself *which are put-downs?*

Listen to those little voices in your head which attack your own self-esteem; the messages you send to yourself at this time in your life that tell you how inadequate, bad, unlovable, etc. you are. Hear how you blame and criticize yourself destructively.

This is another right hand/left hand dialog, as in the previous exercise. Divide the page vertically down the middle. Begin with your writing (dominant) hand in the column on the same side of the page as your hand. Head the column: *Self-put-downs*. Then write out all the put-down messages you send yourself at this particular time in your life. Write them down from the second person, e.g., "You're really incompetent. You'll never get that job." Or "You're no good. You don't deserve to be happy." Or "You're stupid. You'll never achieve your goal."

Read over the self-put-downs. Let your feelings come out by answering back in the empty column on the other side. This time use your other (sub-dominant) hand, as you did in the last exercise.

Uses: This has perhaps been the most powerful exercise in my journal classes, for me and my students. It is an extremely effective tool for confronting a negative self-concept and developing greater self-esteem. Done repeatedly, it can help you overcome self-hatred and doubts about your worth. At the same time you are building an attitude of assertiveness in dealing with destructive criticism from within and without. As Eleanor Roosevelt once said: "Nobody can do anything to me that I'm not already doing to myself." By pinpointing and dealing with attacks on your self-esteem coming from within, you are training yourself to deal with put-downs from others. This is your own private assertive training tool. I used this exercise many times while writing this book and, of course, it worked. (See pages 92 & 93.)

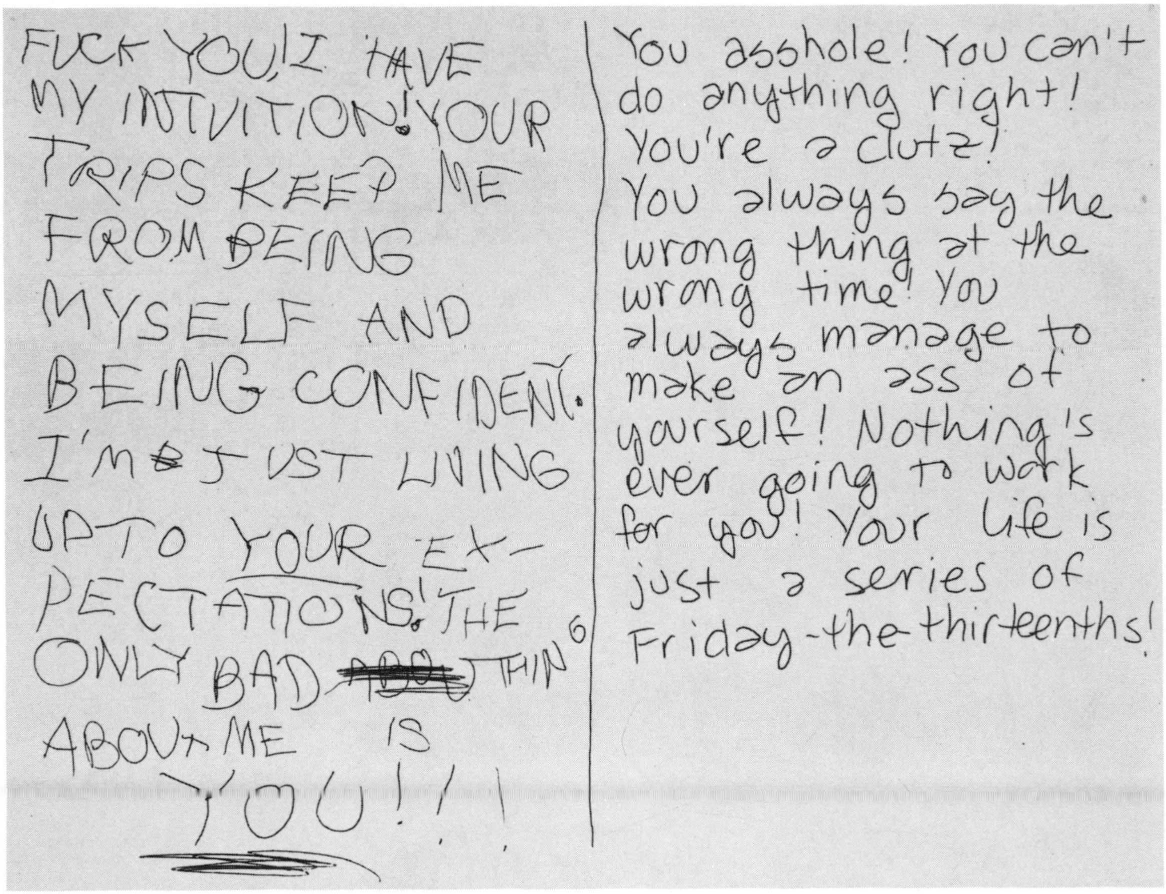

FUCK YOU! I HAVE MY INTUITION! YOUR TRIPS KEEP ME FROM BEING MYSELF AND BEING CONFIDENT. I'M JUST LIVING UP TO YOUR EX-PECTATIONS! THE ONLY BAD THING ABOUT ME IS YOU!!!

You asshole! You can't do anything right! You're a clutz! You always say the wrong thing at the wrong time! You always manage to make an ass of yourself! Nothing's ever going to work for you! Your life is just a series of Friday-the-thirteenths!

Plate 50

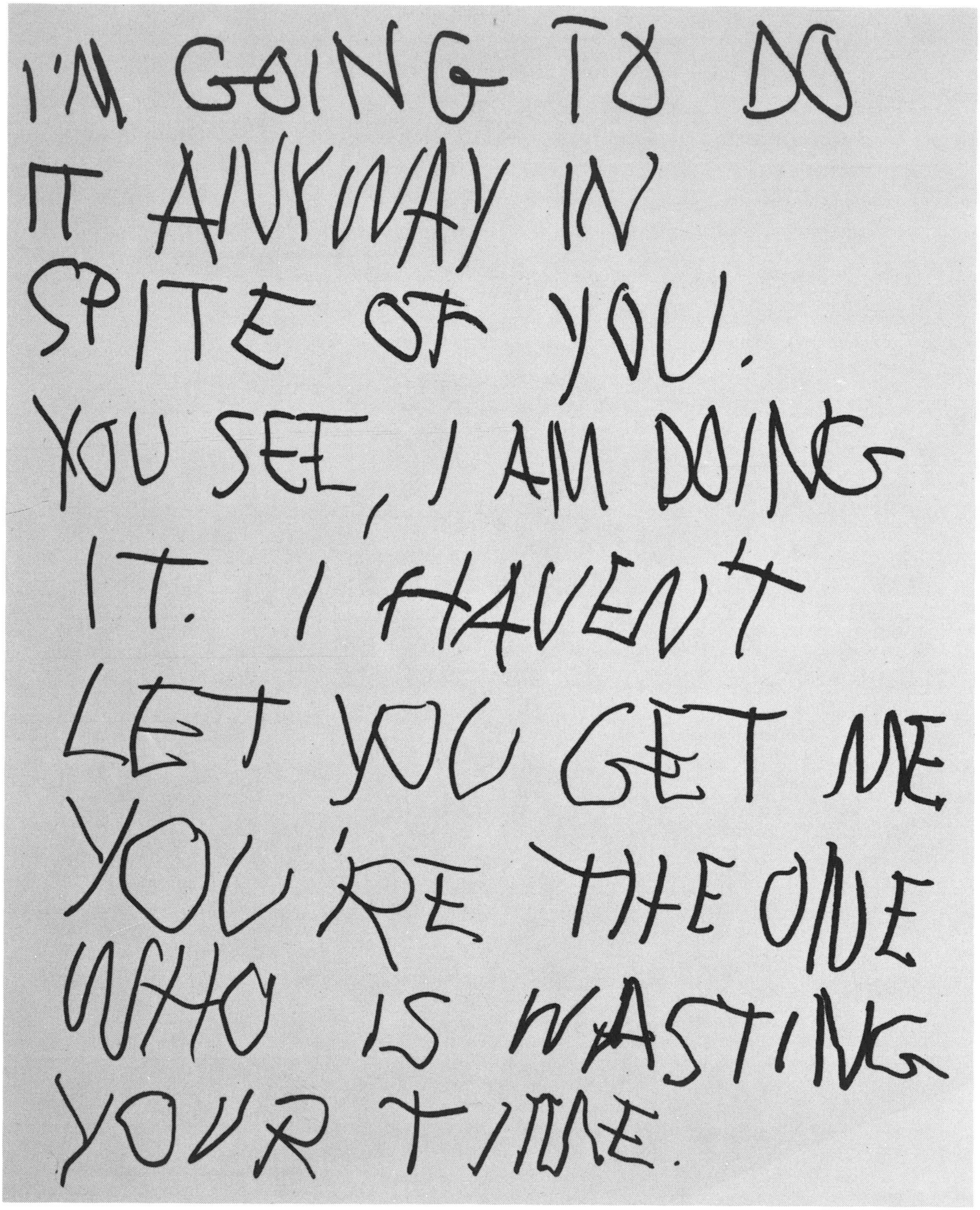

I'M GOING TO DO
IT ANYWAY IN
SPITE OF YOU.
YOU SEE, I AM DOING
IT. I HAVEN'T
LET YOU GET ME
YOU'RE THE ONE
WHO IS WASTING
YOUR TIME.

Plate 51A

You're no author. You can't write.
Look at this stuff you've written.
It's a mess, unclear, dry, garbled.
You're wasting your time.
No publisher is ever going to accept this.

GET LOST
WILL YOU.

Close your eyes and ask yourself:

> *How do I nurture myself? Who are the people and what are the places, things, and activities I choose that are associated with good feelings?*

Visualize yourself enjoying these nurturing elements in your life. Enjoy the feelings of happiness, love, comfort, etc., that are associated with these people, places, things, and activities.

Divide the page into three columns. Make a heading for each as follows:

Nurturing People   *Nurturing Places/Things*   *Nurturing Activities*

In each column list the items in your life that fit that category.

On a new page on the left side, writing with your *sub-dominant hand,* make a heading that says: *I feel weak or vulnerable when . . . .* Complete that sentence as many times as you like, focussing on the states of body, mind, feeling that are associated with feeling "down," such as, physically tired, ill, over-pressured, sad, insecure, etc.

Now, writing with your *dominant* hand, on the right side of the page, respond to the sentences on the left. Answer as your loving, nurturing self. You may want to refer to the items on your list of nurturing aspects above. Your nurturing response might be phrased as follows: "When I feel physically tired . . . *I can rest, listen to music, take a hot bath."* Or it can be stated in the second person: "When you feel tired, I will let you rest." Continue down the list until you have responded lovingly to all the items in the left column.

Uses: This exercise is designed to increase self-love and resources for self-care. Instead of expecting others to read your mind and come to the rescue when you feel down, you can learn to tune in to yourself, assess your needs, and take action to get them met. This may include asking others for help or it may simply be letting yourself *have* whatever feelings you are experiencing, such as sadness, frustration, etc. and expressing them. Hopefully you will learn to treat yourself with tender, loving care if you aren't already.

...my dear Little V. I shall be telling you twice a day or
more that I love you--that you are important to my growth,
that I understand--and that's all that counts--I love you
and am learning how to love you unconditionally. You are
part of me--you are my child and I put my arms around you.
I have given birth to you and you are here. Yes, I know you
will grow up and until or while you do I love you and that's
all that counts, to be loved by me and accepted unconditionally.

Dear God, thank you for the gift of this Dialogue.

A Letter from the Nurturing Self   Plate 52

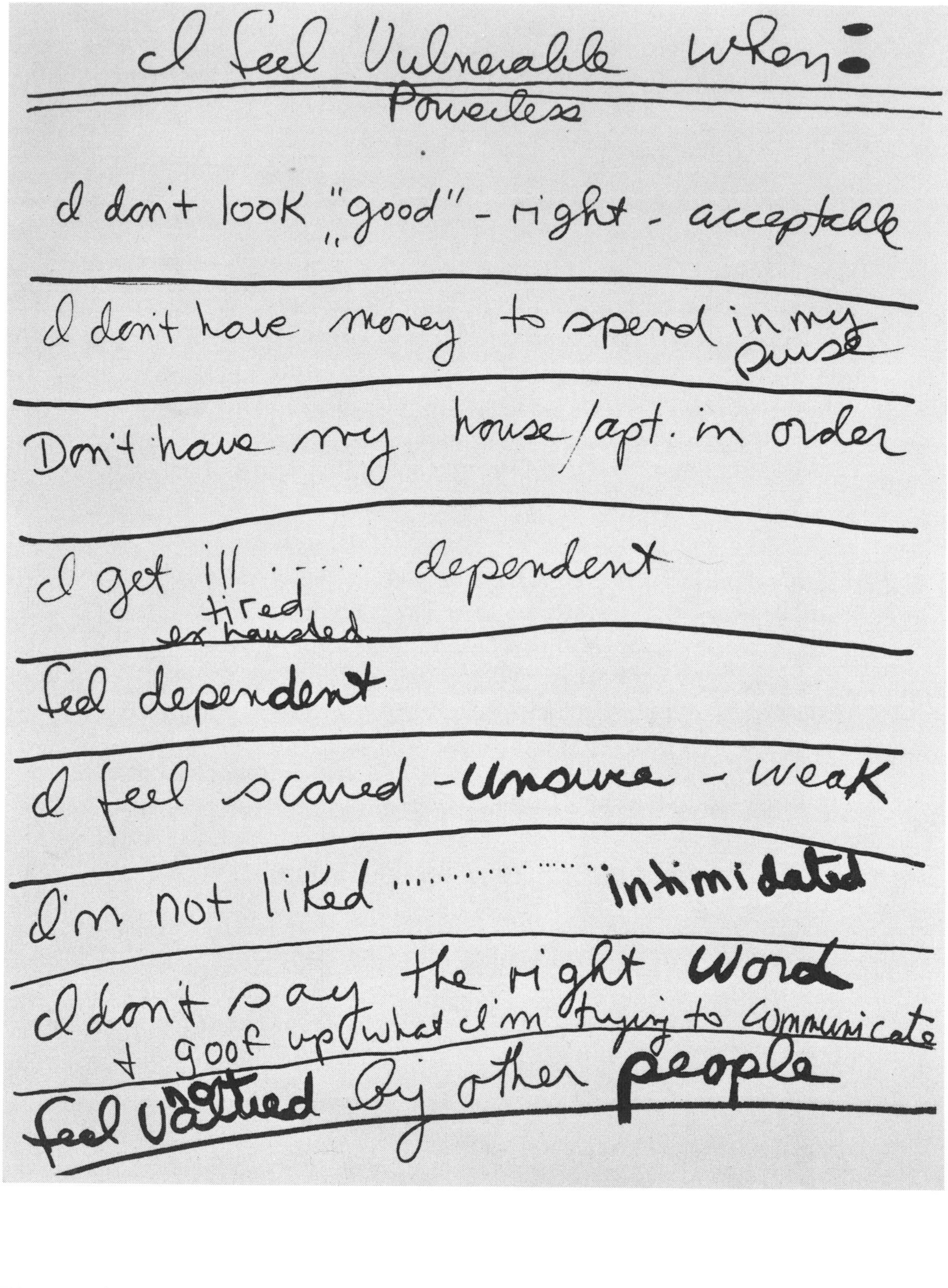

I feel Vulnerable when:
Powerless

I don't look "good" - right - acceptable

I don't have money to spend in my purse

Don't have my house/apt. in order

I get ill ..... dependent
tired
exhausted

feel dependent

I feel scared - unsure - weak

I'm not liked .... intimidated

I don't say the right word
+ goof up what I'm trying to communicate

feel valued by other people

Plate 53A

Nurturing Parent Responds:

I can dress the way I want to . . . .
"funky" to pick up my low spirits
"sloppy" to do my nursery school work
"pretty" to go dancing - - - - - - -
"beautiful" to go to a fancy restaurant

I can buy papayas if I need fruit
I deserve a gift now & then —
I can carry $ . . . . & not spend it - - - - -
it feels good just to have it
I deserve a good movie
I deserve a nice meal out
I deserve an extended telephone connection

Vacuuming once a month is enough for a
small apt.
Dusting is not important
Dirty dishes in the sink is OK . . . .
Dust around the tub & sink is O.K.
messyness can sometimes mean
busyness —

Your body gets tired . . . . . take care of it —
sleep - bathe - relax - listen to
music — put up your feet - have a
massage —

It's human to feel scared at times
we can't been in control of our lives all the time
Regina - relax . . . . & see & feel the love of people around
you —
Your mind is so quick & bright - thats its hard to
talk as fast as you think - slow down —
people do appreciate your thoughtfulness
sincerely - caring

Plate 53B

Meditate upon the following questions:

> *What is important to me in life? What are the essentials that I need for my well-being? What are my priorities?*

Write out a list of your personal needs. Include people, pets, places, things, activities, conditions, etc.

Study your list over to see which needs are not now being met. Put a check next to each of these. You may decide to make some changes in your life toward meeting more of your needs. Write about these changes and how you will implement them. You might turn to page 46 and do the exercise entitled: TIME/LIFE MAP. This can help you in programming the changes into your present schedule.

Uses: Here is an opportunity to really listen to yourself, to practice caring for yourself by becoming aware of your *real* needs. Before we can get our needs met, we have to know what they are. Often, we don't realize that our needs are not being met until it's too late (we become ill, bad-tempered, over-worked, etc.). By keeping this inventory of needs up-to-date, you can avoid some of the negative consequences that result from not taking care of yourself. After all, we are all responsible for knowing our needs and taking action to get them met.

I need. . .
Love above all. . .
   to love myself and be
      a good friend to myself.

I need. . .
to be touched by something
  outside myself
     both physically and spiritually.

I need. . .
to move my body. . .
   to dance
     or do Tai Chi
       or move my body in some way.

I need. . .
to let my creativity out. . .
   to let myself out. . .
     to have an exchange
       with what is around me,
         input and output.

I need air
  and nature
    and to understand and experience
      the origins of the world. . .
        the forests, the life. . .

I need freedom
  to live my life
    as I see fit
      to go outside for walks
        at night if I want. . .
           to run my own existence.

I need. . .
  to be me and be allowed to be me.

Plate 54

YIN AND YANG: THE POLARITIES WITHIN

The words *yin* and *yang* are from the Chinese. *Yin* is receptive and responsive. *Yang* is active, assertive. Traditionally, *yin* has been associated with the so-called "feminine" qualities and *yang* with the "masculine" qualities.

Make two lists, heading one *Yin qualities* and the other *Yang qualities*. In each list, write down the words which express those qualities in yourself. Include both "positive" and "negative" aspects of these traits (ones you like and ones you don't like.)

Meditate upon your lists. Then, using two pages side by side, make two drawings. Let one drawing represent your *yin* qualities and the other drawing express your *yang* qualities, your receptive and your active sides.

Afterward, study the drawings over and write down your thoughts and feelings about them.

Now, make one drawing which integrates both sets of qualities, the *yin* and the *yang* aspects of your personality. Then write down your observations about how it felt to do the drawing and how you perceive the completed design.

Uses: Since we all have both sets of characteristics within us, this is an important tool for balancing. It can pinpoint conflicts or one-sidedness and can help harmonize these aspects toward reaching psychic wholeness and unity, as seen in the yin/yang symbol.

Plate 55

Plate 56A

With an animal on the one side
and a man on the other —
the animal is like an Egyptian Pharaoh —
He is finely tuned, aesthetic & beautiful —
the man is gross & depressed & not
to be trusted. Indeed — the Pharaoh
is the finer part of the part —
the part contains the yin & the yang
the beginning & the end, the male
& the female — Perhaps that which
I most fear is that which I
want the most — Indeed, I too
make a whole which is made
of many parts which are part of
a whole which is Me

Close your eyes and turn your attention inward. Think about the human personality traits which you observe in others and experience in yourself. Ask yourself:

> *What does the* bright side *look like? What are the qualities I like in myself? What qualities do I admire in others and wish I had?*

Then ask yourself:

> *What does the* shadow side *look like? What are the human traits that I fear, dislike, and criticize in myself and/or in others?*

Choose two colors, one for each hand. Let one color/hand express the *bright side* (qualities you like); let the other color/hand express the *shadow side* (traits you don't like). Now, draw your impression, using both hands at the same time or alternately. You might want to write some of the names of these characteristics into your drawing.

Uses: Here is a tool for exploring your so-called positive/negative sides, the good/bad, beautiful/ugly polarities that live side by side as partners inside each one of us. This exercise is designed to help you see yourself as you really are and, hopefully, lead the way toward self-acceptance and acceptance of others as they are (not as you would like them to be.)

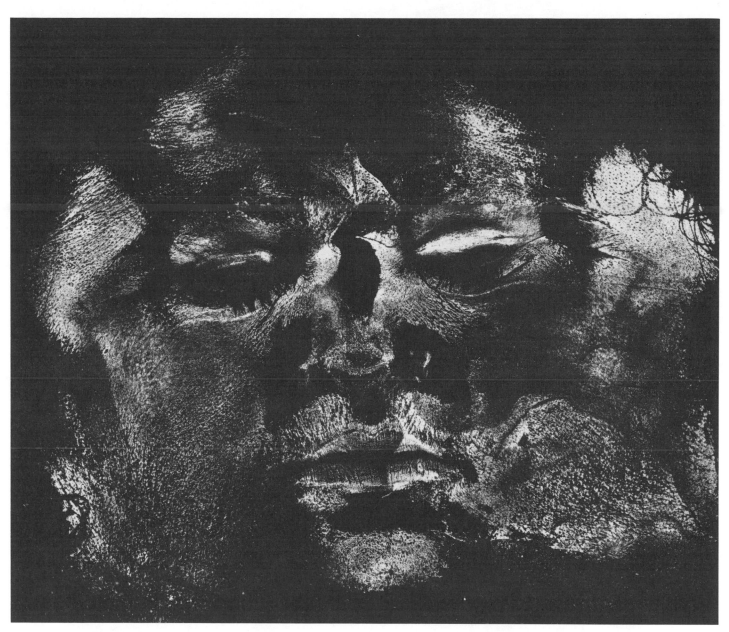

I've been working in the darkroom making vaseline prints. The effect is an inner self portrait. Three of my parts emerge from the shadowy depths. The wise inner-guide, Xanadu, is there. Fragile, emotional Genieve quakes in her boots and, of course, my raging monster, Batswinger, is present. I own them all, they make up my shadow. I can see them all in this print.

Plate 57

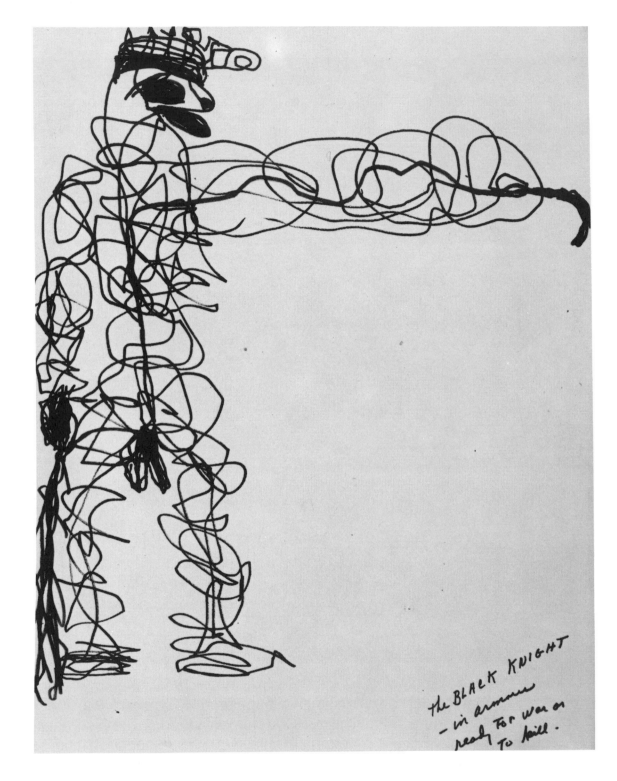

the BLACK KNIGHT
– in armour
ready for war or
to kill.

Plate 58A

Plate 58B

Plate 59A

What do you want from me?

(S) I want you to hold me—to love me, to respect me, to cherish me, to come into my places, my home—to comfort me, to always stay with me, to take loving care of me, to do lots and lots of things for me—give me your light, give me your guidance, love me, respect me.

Ugh—I hate all that dependency—Damn—can't you take care of yourself instead of wanting me to do it all the time? God—

(S) I'm too scared.

Ugh.

(S) I know you find me repulsive. I wish I weren't. I want you to see that I'm beautiful.

What's beautiful about you? What can you do for me?

(S) I can guide you in the basement. I can help you find your gut feelings and use them. I can help you find your way out of here. I can be very clever.

Scared, scared, scared spider. God—why can't you speak for yourself instead of being so damn obtuse. Damn! I'm impatient with your process—your slowness, your stupidity. Damn. I don't want to read your mind—I don't want to *work* so hard when I'm with you. I work with clients (in therapy). I don't want to work with friends. I need friends who have higher states of consciousness, who speak for themselves.

(S) You can't get rid of me! I live here. You either have to own me and hold me or be poisoned by me. I have lots of sting. See! Lots of toxicity.

Plate 59B

Think about the personality traits which you do not like. Focus on your *shadow side* and ask about each of these aspects of yourself:

> *How do I behave and communicate when I express this trait? How do I treat others? How do I feel inside? What situations prompt or trigger me into "playing this part" or adopting this behavior?*

Using a double page spread, head one side: *The Selves I Don't Like.* Then with each one, do the following:

a) Personality trait. Give it a name. For instance, your rigid, doctrinaire aspect might appear as "Professor Know-it-all" (see example below).

b) Describe yourself and how you behave when you are playing that role. Introduce yourself in the first person, e.g., "I'm Professor Know-it-all and I have all the answers. Don't contradict me because I'm always right."

c) Tell how you really feel inside when you are into that particular role.

d) Tell which situations or people trigger or cue you into playing that role.

Do this for as many unacceptable traits as you want to explore at this time.

On the other side of the double page spread, repeat the exercise, heading the page: *The Selves I Do Like.* Personify each trait, giving it a name and letting it speak for itself, telling how it behaves, feels, and what situations and people are associated with it. You might also want to let the *Do Like* "characters" speak to the *Don't Like* ones.

Uses: This is a further explanation of the many aspects of your personality and how they express themselves in everyday life. You can learn to recognize the "characters" within you, their style of behavior and motivation. If you pause and reflect on the parts you *Don't Like,* you might get to the heart of what's causing the behavior, what you are covering up, trying to prove, protect, or avoid. If you can see through your little games, you are then free to choose more honest and direct ways of relating. If you can own up to the *real* feelings underneath the disguise or role, you may wish to share them with others instead of play-acting.

Not O.K. Self

Professor Know-it-all

I'm in charge. I know what I'm talking about. Don't contradict me or I'll rationalize my way around you to come out looking good—right.

I behave in a dictatorial, pompous, arrogant manner. I can be argumentative and full of B.S.

I feel (deep inside) threatened, hurt pride, ashamed of not really knowing everything.

O.K. Self

Illuminata

I have a lot of wisdom and I express myself clearly, articulately, sensitively from the guts and heart.

I don't pretend to "know" everything. I share openly from my own life experience, knowing what is right for me but not imposing on others. I am tolerant of other people as they are. I trust my own feelings and intuitions as my personal guide. I respect that others may not agree or see things as I do and I'm accepting of that.

Plate 60

Picture your body in your mind's eye. Meditate on each area as you did in the relaxation meditation on Page 16. As you inventory your body, experience your physical sensations and feelings. If you discover pain or discomfort in any area, pause and focus on the sensations in that part. Visualize that body part and how it appears right now. If you're not sure what it looks like, e.g., internal organs, then use your imagination.

Draw the outline of your body and then color in the area(s) of pain, tension, or other discomfort. Or simply draw the body part(s) or organ(s) that you want to focus on.

Now, speak to each body part or area. Ask it:

> *How do you feel? What caused you to feel this way? What can I do for you?*

Let the body part respond and write down your conversation.

Draw the body part in the image of its healthy, well state as you picture that to be in your imagination.

Uses: This dialog and visualization of your body parts can get you into better relationship with yourself as living in physical form. By listening to your body messages (symptoms) regularly, you can practice real self-care and prevent problems from getting worse. Here is a way to put creative imagination to work in the service of well-being.

B. I am your bladder and I don't like the way you are holding back on me. You're not being honest with me.

Well, I'm angry.

B. So you're angry. Why don't you tell me what you're angry about?

Because I'm just one ball of fury and it's very frightening to me to be so angry.

B. Well, it doesn't help me any for you to fill me up with your anger. If you'd just let some of it out at the time you feel it, instead of holding it in, then the poison wouldn't all back up in me.

I'm not sure you'd love me if you knew how angry I was.

B. Love you, why I'd be able to love you more. It's your anger that keeps us apart.

But I need that anger because I'm afraid of being too close.

B. What would it mean to you if we did get too close?

Then you'd get to know all about me. Especially the rotten part.

B. I don't know of any rotten part.

I know you don't, but I do and I have to live with it every day of my life.

B. You mean the part that failed to succeed?

Why yes, how did you know?

B. Why I've known all the time but that doesn't make me love you less.

Do you really mean that?

B. Of course I do. I have succeeded to fail and you failed to succeed. I really don't understand success and failure anyway.

I guess I don't either. That sure makes me feel better. There is much too much energy spent on success and failure. I guess I've been too intense about it. It's a good feeling not to have to be concerned or worry whether I'm succeeding or failing all the time.

It kind of reminds me of school and being concerned about my grades and whether I passed or failed that particular class.

B. Yeh, the pressure was terrible. I'm glad we don't get grades on our knowledge or performance today.

Geez, can you believe the pressures we put on ourselves today when we don't have to.

B. I'm glad we had this talk because I sure feel a lot better. Thanks.

Plate 61

LOVE LETTER TO MYSELF

Meditate upon all the things about yourself that you love. Then write a letter to yourself in which you describe the qualities and ways of being that you love in yourself.

Uses: This is a method of affirming your own worth and building up self-esteem. By learning to love yourself you are increasing your ability to love others. This kind of self-appreciation is not to be confused with egotism or self-centeredness which discounts the feelings and needs of others. True self-love is expansive and leads to openness and contact with others. If you feel good about yourself, you will find it far easier to feel good about others.

Dear Self:
I love you and sometimes I don't show it. But I really do underneath it all and you know it, too. Underneath all the hard times, I have been faithful to you. And, of course, I'm very proud of you. You are a lovely person, and friend to me. You are never boring—but always alive, interested, curious, growing—You are deep and broad.
I love you.

Plate 62

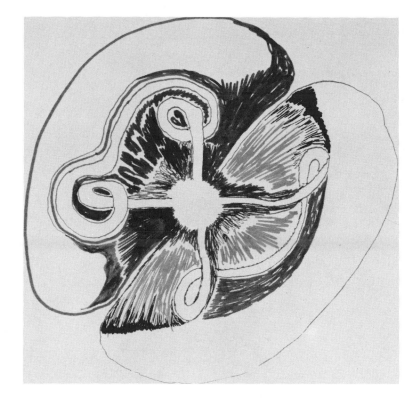

Hold me, echoes the whisper from within
Hold me near you
Hold me close to your heart
as the apple of your eye

Through the distant chambers of time
our hearts beat
as the wings of doves
brush against the skies of eternity

We were never parted
for we are one through infinite
space and time

You have embraced me in shadow
unbeknownst to my daytime self,
always present behind me,
above me, beneath.

You are the ground of my existence
forever with and within me.

Plate 63

"We're like a couple of kids—We hold each other and hold on to each other. We're safe."

Plate 64

"Only those who have already experienced a revolution within themselves can reach out effectively to help others."

—Malcolm X

"Keep your heart in wonder at the daily miracles of your life."

—Kahlil Gibran

5   How You Are With Others: People, Places and Things

You have been exploring the private reality of your inner space. Now it is time to view your relationship to the world around you and the people, places, and things that make up your personal environment. You'll examine your connection with the elements that surround you every day and see how they live inside you. You'll also have an opportunity to study your system of values and beliefs as they are expressed outwardly and see yourself from some new angles.

These exercises are intended to help you:

- see the context in which you live
- clarify your feelings about others
- explore and expand your relationships with others
- develop clearer communication with others
- enrich your resources and strengthen your support system
- examine the significance of the elements in your personal world
- define needs and desired changes in relation to the world around you

A VERY IMPORTANT PERSON

Focus in on your life at the present time and ask:

> *Who is the most important person in my life right now? How do I feel about this person?*

This could be someone you know or someone you have never met but who has influenced you in an important way. It could be someone you are on good terms with or someone with whom you are in conflict. Close your eyes and let the person's image appear before you. Let yourself feel the quality of his or her presence. Really BE WITH the person in your imagination.

Draw a graphic expression of your relationship with this person. Create an image that reflects the quality of connection between you at this time.

Write a letter to the person, sharing your feelings about the relationship *as it is now* and *as you would like it to be*. Review the past in your relationship, if you wish, and what it has meant to you. This is not intended as a letter to be sent, so don't edit or slant your remarks as though the individual were listening. Be as honest as possible.

Variation: Imagine other things which are important to you at this time in your life, such as: other significant people, your work, important places, objects, etc. Create a graphic image for each one and then write to or about it.

Uses: This exercise is a tool for understanding how your inner life is affected by people, things and situations in your personal world. It can be especially helpful in situations where communication with another person or element in your life has broken down and you've been unable to clarify your true feelings. Often, this exercise can bring out an articulation of feelings in a way that can later be communicated to the other person, either in a letter *which you do send* or in face to face contact.

graph of my relationship with the VIP in my life today.

Graph of my relationship with the V.I.P. in my life today.

The graph shows my relationship with Jimmy and all the many threads that are interwoven in our relationship. Bold colors, no "downer" colors in the relationship. The threads of color that pass back and forth between us are vibrant. Vibrant means "good vibes."
There's charisma, there is a flowing, and it is free and flowing and not rigid.
He is the most important person in my life today.

Plate 65A

120   Dear Jimmy,

How do I begin to tell you what you mean to me? To me you mean boldness, strength, forthrightness, courage, a love of life and people. You're not a person who just wants a taste of life, you want a big bite of life. Perhaps even more than your share. But maybe it's because you can handle more than most people.

I see you with your "bear hugs" wanting to embrace the world, and hugging it to you. Maybe even saying "This is mine, all mine." Maybe in your youthful exuberance that is most acceptable for now and you have that right to hold what you love dearly so close to you. But I would suggest temperance because in your great strength you could crush that which you hold most dear only because you may not be aware that some things are fragile and, although love has such great strength, love is also fragile.

Love,

Mother

Plate 65B

Think back over your life and ask yourself:

> *Which people have had the biggest influence on my life? Who are the people I have admired and emulated? Who have been my models, gurus and guides, my heroic figures?*

These may have been relatives, friends, teachers. They may have been public figures or fictional characters from plays, books, movies, etc. They may have been famous people from history, myth, or legend. Close your eyes and visualize these people who were important influences on your life. Think about the qualities and characteristics they signify for you: values, knowledge, personality, and physical traits.

Choose one of your heroic figures or models and focus on that individual. Close your eyes and imagine the person standing before you. See and feel the presence of this very important person in your life. In your imagination, share your feelings with the individual. Tell him or her what the nature of the influence has been and how you feel about it. Then ask the person for guidance relating to your current concerns or a particular problem or challenge you are facing. Let your V.I.P. respond in your imagination. Write down the conversation in your journal. If you wish, draw a picture or symbolic expression of the person.

Uses: When you need to tap into inner wisdom, this exercise can provide an excellent vehicle. The people you have chosen to emulate live on within you. Their qualities in you can be helpful guides whenever you need them.

Journal entry after coming home from the Anaïs Nin 2/21/77
celebration in Los Angeles in honor of her death and birthday. 11:50 PM

No Tears for Anaïs

There were no tears tonight—
for you,
great lady of the waters,
needed none.
You had done what you came to do
and more
Flashing the light of your words
through the psychic gold mines
buried so deep within us all.

No tears for the living or dead, tonight.
What was there to cry about?
You had lived life fully
and left a trail of jewels
like blossoms dropping from the trees in spring
scattered there on your path
for us to follow, to find and to study
And in so doing
we follow the path into ourselves
as you showed us how to do.

What on earth is there to cry about,
or in heaven, for that matter?

No, there were no tears for you or for us,
tonight, Anaïs.
We had seen too much
in your eyes and through them
to ever profane your memory
with tears

No, not tonight, Anaïs
No tears
Only goodnight
Anaïs

Plate 66

This is me and my mother. She is like a cup that I came out of.
But I'm also around the sides of her, too. When I lived at home
we used to take naps together like "spoons." (We still do sometimes.)
There's lots of tenderness and flow in this picture. We're both
surrounded by our purple spirituality and mysticism. I got this
from her. Beyond the purple is the sea and the moon--symbols of
our womanhood.

Plate 67

MY SUPPORT SYSTEM

Think about the people in your life and ask:

> *Who are the people I turn to in time of need when I want understanding, encouragement, support, assistance of any kind?*

Think of these people as your personal support system. Picture them in your imagination and experience the feelings you have about them.

Create a graphic design or picture of yourself and all the individuals and groups that make up your support system. You can label each element in the drawing by name. Then write down how each person provides support.

Study your support system carefully. If you see a need to strengthen your network of supportive elements by adding to or enriching it, write down ways in which you will go about doing this.

Uses: This is an important tool for assessing your resources (or lack of them) and for strengthening your supports. If you find that your support system is weak or that you rely too heavily on only one or two people, you can take steps to expand your network. It is very reassuring to know that you are not alone and that you can get help when you need it. But it is up to you to create your own network of supportive people; individuals who really accept and care about you. Learning to seek genuine nurturing and help from others reflects the fact that you care about yourself.

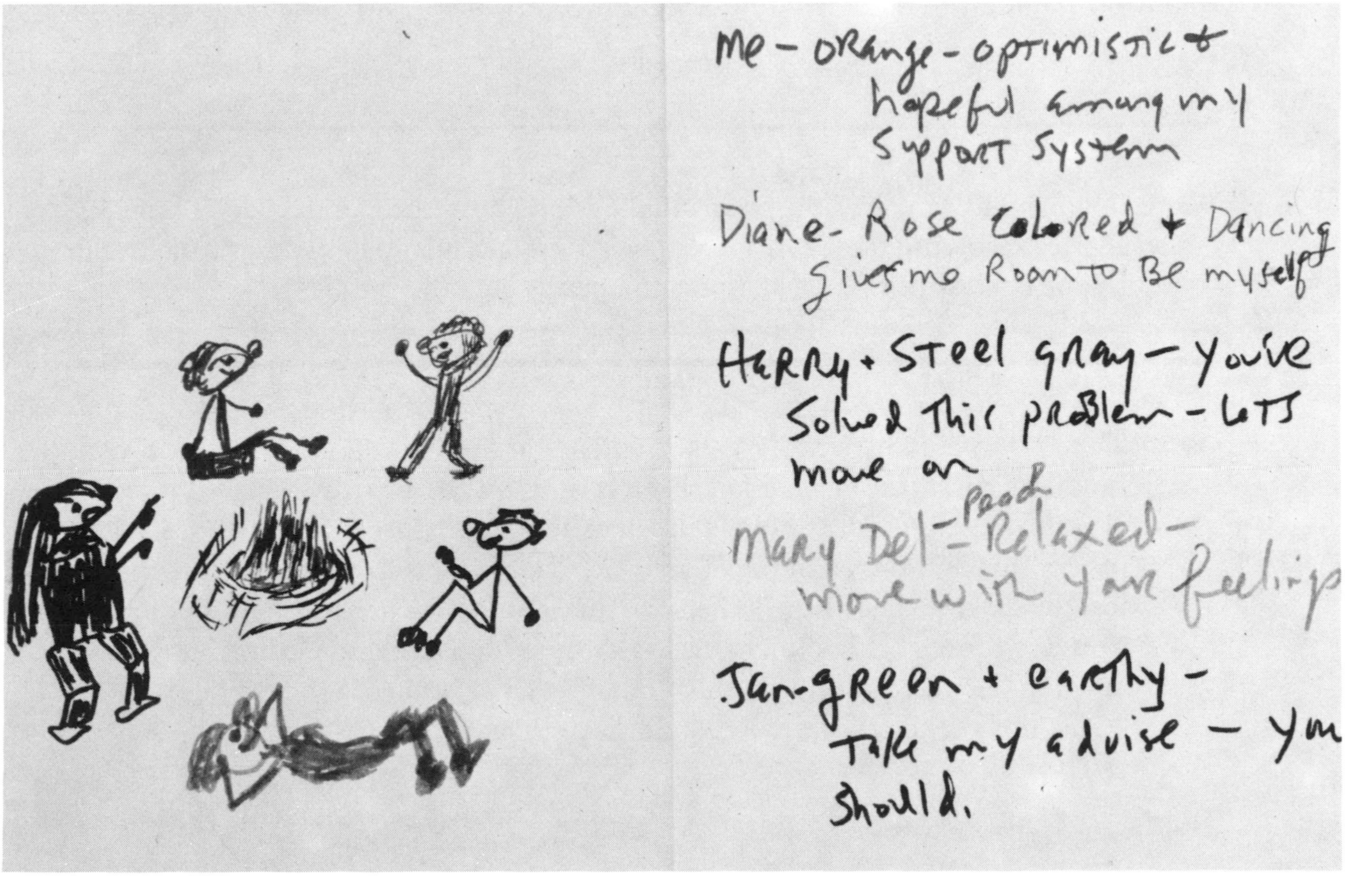

Me - oRange - optimistic &
hopeful among my
Support System

Diane - Rose coloRed & Dancing
Gives me Room to Be myself

HARRY & Steel gray - you've
Solved This problem - LeTS
move on

Mary Del - Relaxed -
move with your feelings

Jan - gReen & earthy -
Take my advise - you
should.

Plate 68

Visualize a significant person in your life. Picture the person as he/she is at the present time. Think about the personality trait or quality you feel is lacking or weak in this person. Then ask yourself:

What quality do I wish this person had?

A quality may have come to mind, such as: sense of humor, open-mindedness, patience. Meditate upon the quality or characteristic for awhile. Now, imagine giving the desired quality to this person. Visualize him or her possessing the quality. Imagine the person's new appearance, behavior, attitude after receiving the gift of this quality from you.

Write down what you saw in your imagination: how the person looks, speaks, behaves after receiving the quality you have given as a gift. Use the present tense in writing your description, *as if* the person already has the quality.

Uses: This exercise is especially useful when you are having difficulty in a relationship with another person. By focusing on the positive desired quality, you can develop that trait in yourself. Then YOU possess it and *can* give it to others through the example of your own behavior and attitude. You will be less likely to expect from others qualities that you are not living yourself. You can't force others to change, but you do have the power to change and develop desired qualities within yourself. To paraphrase the Biblical quote: "*Give* unto others what you would have them *give* unto you."

In my art therapy session last week with my client, Sarah, I guided her through the "Giving unto Others" exercise. She pictured her estranged husband, Roberto. When it came to giving him a quality, she chose "honesty." Here's what she said.

Sarah: "Honesty. That is what I would like to give him. I see him right now as going with a fad, of not being his real self. I pictured him as his face would appear transformed by honesty, his features chiseled and clear.

I can give him that gift by being honest, by being that way myself when I am with him on Saturday for his first visit in two months and by seeing him as he really is now."

A few days after that session, Sarah had a meeting with Roberto and told him that she felt it was time to get a divorce. She wanted to finish it up. She reported having done most of the talking. Roberto was very quiet, she said, and she had felt very calm and strong. She had increased self-confidence after that meeting with Roberto. She said she had been more honest with him, had given him the "gift" of honesty which she'd done in the fantasy in our recent session. She said she felt much stronger for it. Also, she felt better and more realistic about who Roberto really is. When she had spoken of divorce in previous meetings with him, he had avoided the discussion. This time he listened to her feelings. She was also more honest in expressing them, too.

Plate 69

(Note: names have been changed for this passage from my journal to maintain confidentiality)

THE MOST SATISFYING RELATIONSHIP

Think about the relationships you've had in your life and ask yourself:

Who is the person with whom I've had the most satisfying relationship?

Let that person appear in your mind's eye and meditate upon him or her for awhile. Experience your feelings about the relationship: what it was like being together and what the other person means to you. (This can be anyone, living or dead.) Picture some of the experiences you've had with this person.

_____

Draw a graphic representation of your relationship with this person.

_____

Write a letter to the person telling how you feel, describe the qualities you value in him/her, what the relationship means to you and how you would like it to be in the future.

_____

Uses: Here is a way to understand and appreciate relatedness to another. Truly satisfying relationships are treasures in our lives and can teach us a great deal about ourselves and what we value in our connections with other human beings.

SOMEONE I'D LIKE TO KNOW

Close your eyes and create an imaginary person. Let this person be someone you'd like to know. This is an individual drawn from your own imagination, just as a novelist or playwright creates a character. Visualize the person standing in front of you. Get a clear picture of his/her physical characteristics, clothing, and so on. Get a feeling for the individual's personality. Let the person introduce him/herself by name.

Now, imagine the setting and circumstances of this, your first meeting with this person. Then have an imaginary conversation in which your new acquaintance tells about him/herself. Ask questions, make any comments. Write the conversation out as the dialog in a play script.

Uses: This is an exercise in creative imagination. As mentioned above, you are doing what any writer does in creating a character for a story or play. You are also exploring some of your own qualities. Some of your own characteristics (or ones that you wish you had) may emerge as you "project" or personify these in this fictional person you've created. By bringing these qualities to light, you are tapping some of your hidden potential.

MY OWN SPACE

Close your eyes. Picture the environment in which you live (your room, apartment, house). Take an imaginary walk through the space(s). Pretend you are a stranger visiting the place for the first time. See what the environment reflects about the person or people who live here.

Write down your impressions. What does the place say about its inhabitants?

Draw a floorplan, then write out what each room would say if it could speak. Let it speak in the first person, singular: "I'm the kitchen . . ."

Write down your reactions to what you've written and drawn. Are there any changes you wish to make? What are they, how can you implement them?

Variation: If you are sharing a dwelling with others, focus on your own personal space, the area that is yours and expresses your personality. Do the exercise above, applying it to your own space. Apply this exercise to other kinds of space: car, office, etc.

Uses: This exercise enables you to see the connection between the "space you're in" inside (feelings, attitudes) and the space you create around you. If you don't like what your environment says about you, you can change it to create an atmosphere that is more satisfying. This is also a good tool for examining the nature of relationships between you and those with whom you live, work, etc.

As I walk into this house I feel a quietness. The people that live here like color.
The lady of this house likes elegance as indicated by the candles on the dining
table. The chairs and sofa are comfortable and the plants show some neglect in
some and others seem to be flourishing but not to any great extent. The pictures
are merely pleasant, quite traditional and no special flair for artistic expression.
The most expressive part is the air of comfort, not ostentatious nor extravagant.
Fairly middle class except for the boldness in using color. It is quite conservative,
the type of magazines and literature around doesn't tell me that these people are
terribly intellectual but really have quite simple taste in their reading matter.

The bedroom is quite simple and doesn't express any passionate feelings, more
functional than romantic. The den shows there might be some flurry of activity
here but I don't see signs of any hobbies. It seems fairly feminine but simple and
practical enough to know that a man lives here but doesn't spend too much time
here. There aren't too many signs of him in the house other than his toiletries in
the bathroom and his pajamas on the back of the door.

The few photos around show that there was more to the family and they have
recently grown and are out of the house by their pictures and the fact that there is
no evidence of children. The house is clean and neat but not too lived in. It seems a
little too sterile and only the colors keep it from being so.

The furniture is not worn so one doesn't have a sense of any past. There are few
people that come to this house. It is mainly for the two that live in it. The people
that come, come to eat.

Plate 70

MY FAVORITE THINGS

Think about all of your favorite things, the objects which are most significant to you. They may be "prized possessions" or associated with satisfying experiences. They may be plants, pets, objects. As you think about these things, ask yourself:

What is my favorite thing at the present time in my life?

Close your eyes and visualize your favorite thing. Picture it clearly, seeing its colors, shape, texture, form. Think about its function in your life, how you use it, and what it means to you. Recall how it came into your life, the circumstances of your first encounter with it and how you acquired it (if you own it).

Draw a picture of your favorite thing. Use your memory or look at it while you draw. Relax and take your time. You are not being judged for artistic skill. Rather you are fondly showing your appreciation of your favorite thing by taking the time to study it lovingly and draw it with care. Drawing, here, is a kind of dialog with the cherished object.

Now, imagine that the object can talk. Imagine what it would say. Let it tell you about itself, what it wants from you, what it wants *for* you. Write the dialog out.

Study your drawing and dialog and then write down your reactions.

Uses: This is a way to explore still another facet of yourself as reflected in your outer environment. It also develops powers of observation.

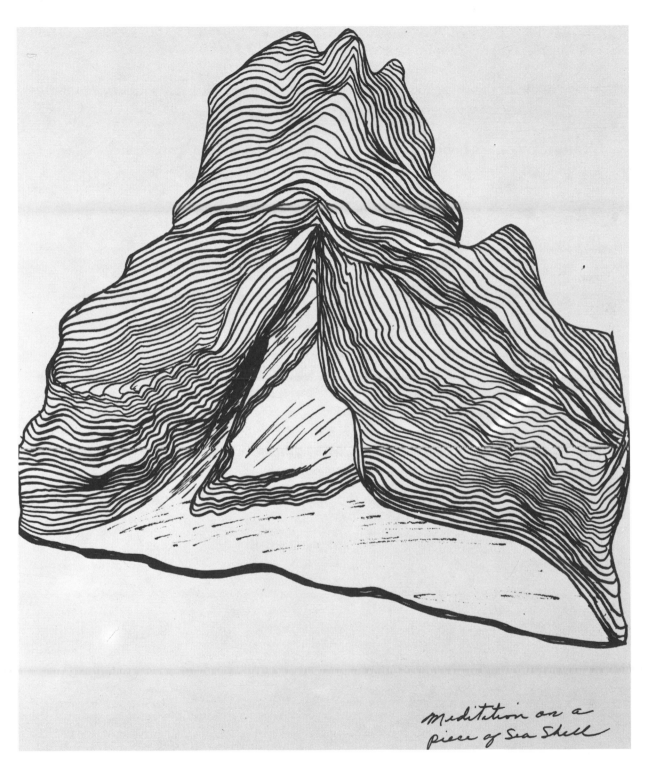

Meditation on a
piece of Sea Shell

Plate 71

When you have read a book, seen a film or play, a painting or other work of art that has impressed you deeply, ask yourself:

What meaning does it have for me? What insights have I gained and how can I apply them in my everyday life?

If you are reading a book that is important to you, you might want to write passages of it in your journal.

Write or draw your reflections.

Uses: This is a means to enrich and deepen your experience of works of art which contain elements that mirror back your own inner wisdom. Works of art are vessels for universal human understanding and awareness and by meditating on them we spark our own creative spirit.

The example on the next page is a drawn reflection on a quote from the book, *Mary Barnes: Two Accounts of a Journey Through Madness*, by Mary Barnes and Joseph Berke. The words are:

"In order to come to the light
   I have to germinate in the dark."

Mary Barnes

"In order to come to the light
we have to germinate in the "dark.""

May Barnes

2/15/66

Plate 72

Plate 73

"Follow you the star that lights a desert pathway, yours or mine, forward till you see the Highest Human Nature is divine."

—Alfred Lord Tennyson

A God Within is a translation of the original Greek phrase from which the word ENTHUSIASM comes.

6 What Your Higher Self Knows

We all carry within us rich sources of wisdom. Often, this wisdom speaks to us in its own language of symbols as revealed in dreams, fantasies, and poetic imagery. However, this kind of symbolism seems strange and mysterious to most people in our culture and they dismiss things such as dreams and fantasies as being irrational, meaningless. So, most of our dreams are like elusive, ethereal butterflies that flutter by in the night only to vanish when we open our eyes to daylight. The first exercises in the chapter focus on dream recall and documentation. Like butterfly nets, they are tools for capturing dream symbols for closer observation. The techniques for de-coding these symbols are like magnifying glasses and microscopes enabling you to study the images and experiences of your dream world in all their details and dimensions, bringing the messages of the creative unconscious into the light. These are followed by exercises in imagination and intuition that can put you in touch with the wise person that lives within you.

These techniques are designed to help you:

- explore your intuition, imagination, and creativity
- discover and understand your personal symbolism
- make sense out of the messages from your higher self
- value and be true to the voices of wisdom within you
- see the relationship between intuitive insight and daily life
- express and apply your unique understanding and the wisdom from your higher self

PREPARING FOR DREAM EXPLORATION

Remembering your dreams

Many people say they don't dream or can't remember their dreams. If you *want* to remember your dreams, you can train yourself to do so. Here are some simple techniques for dream recall.

1. *Practice auto-suggestion before going to sleep.*

   As you drift off to sleep, say to youself:

   > *I'm going to remember my dreams when I wake up.*

   Then let yourself float off to dream land. Don't worry about whether you'll succeed or not. Just relax and go to sleep. If you don't recall your dreams at first, continue this auto-suggestion every night anyway until your dreams *do* start coming through. Many of my journal students report that they are flooded with dreams after using this technique. Planting seeds (the wish to remember dreams) in the unconscious mind during that twilight zone between waking and sleeping can yield a rich harvest of consciously remembered dreams.

2. *Upon waking, review the dream before opening your eyes.*

   Go over the dream in your mind's eye as soon as you wake up but before opening your eyes. Remember as much as you can. It's as though you were playing back a movie. It helps to "fix" the dream in your memory by giving it a title. Then focus on the highlights: key people, places, objects, events, experiences, visual impressions. This review is a quick, condensed version of the dream, somewhat like the coming attractions for a feature length film. It is important that you do this before opening your eyes and becoming distracted by the outer world. Again, in this transition state between sleep and waking, there is greater access to the unconscious and to the dream world. If you get up at this point and start your regular activities before reviewing the dream, chances are good that the dream will vanish.

Write or draw the dream in your journal or tape record it (to be transcribed later into your journal). Do this as soon as possible after you review(#2 above) so that you don't get distracted with other thoughts or input from outside. If you must delay documenting the dream fully, then at least jot down a quick outline of the highlights to freeze it in your memory.

If you document your dream verbally (written or spoken into a tape recorder), speak in the present tense as though you are reliving the dream. This gives it more immediacy. If you can't recall the entire dream but fragments of it are coming through as visual images, then draw them or describe them in writing. When documenting your dream, do not analyze, editorialize, or interpret its meaning. Just get the raw material down. Save your reactions and interpretations for later, when you "process" the dream in depth with the exercises contained in this chapter. You may wish to do the dream exploration work later on when more time is available. Dream work can often take quite awhile, depending on the length, intricacy, or power of the dream and upon your desire to delve into it.

You can explore a dream with one or more of the following exercises, choosing the ones that seem most appropriate for de-coding that particular dream. Once you have trained yourself to recall and document your dreams, you need not do it regularly unless you want to focus on dreams for a particular period of time or find that a dream is coming through loud and clear and is asking for attention. These techniques are simply given as tools to prepare you to explore your dreams whenever you wish to do so.

THE DREAM SPEAKS

Write out your dream as it happened, preferably in the present tense. Don't interpret or editorialize, simply document what happened.

_____

Read it over and write down any first thoughts and feelings regarding the meaning of the dream. See if there are any areas of your life that it might be pointing to or speaking about symbolically.

_____

Underline the key elements in your written record of the dream. Let each one speak to you, telling its name, its thoughts and feelings, its qualities, what it was doing in your dream and what it wants from you or for you.

_____

If the dream seems to be speaking about a specific issue in your life, then write further about that.

_____

Uses: This exercise provides a tool for examining the symbolic forms and events in dreams and for relating these symbols to everyday life situations. By identifying with the elements (getting inside them and speaking for them), you can gain a deeper understanding of how they represent parts of yourself. The _story_ of the dream may indicate one issue in your life or one layer of experience, the conversations with the parts might uncover still another level of meaning. Digging into dreams is like doing a geological survey, with many strata of symbolic messages dwelling under the surface of the dream plot.

Had a dream last night:

"Pathways of the Heart"

In London, trying to get to where I live on the subway, the Underground. I was lost, and couldn't figure out where I was, or where to transfer. I hadn't said anything, or asked anybody directions. I started to get off at a stop I thought might be a transfer point, and the conductor asked me where I was going. When I told him, he said "You can't get there from here." He pulled out a map, which turned out to be a diagram of a heart. He said the system was like a heart, and that if I would travel the pathways of the heart, I would get wherever I needed to go!

What a far-out dream! This dream does not really require interpretation — it is more like a clear instruction. It is telling me to stay with the energy of my heart, open my heart chakra, and if I do, everything will just flow! So far, I've lived most of my life in my head. Actually, all my life. Time to move to my heart!

Plate 74

Dream again last night (two in a row — amazing)

Driving down the *freeway* and it's *pitch dark.* I don't see anything around me but I know the *sea* is to my right. All of a sudden I see a *car accident* up ahead. My braking distance is very short. I slam on the *brakes.* The possibility of piling into the other cars seems very real. The other cars are at *right angles* to one another. The car that is perpendicular to the road is a *white '56 Chevy.* The other car is a green *Packard.* I stop just feet behind the Packard. The destruction of the whole thing frightens me. I wake up.

I am the freeway. I am solid and provide a straight path that can be
traveled on.
I am the dark. I represent the unknown and fear.
I am the sea which is emotional, powerful and rhythmic.
I am the car accident which is destruction and pain.
I am the brakes which can stop movement.
I am the right angles which are at cross purposes with one another.
My purpose is to present an obstacle.
I am the white '56 Chevy which is shiny and polished. I am well
taken care of and my purpose is to carry young people with hopes and dreams.
I am a dark green Packard which is old, over-stuffed, and clunky. My
purpose is to carry families.

What the dream means

I'm on a path and it is not clear where it will end up. The process of change and movement to a new place is frightening to me. Part of me wants to get beyond the obstacles into a new space. Another part strongly resists change. The part that resists in me is stuck with the ancient fears of the past. I need to mend the broken pieces before I can go on.

Plate 75

If you don't like the way a dream unfolded or ended, you can change it. After all, it is YOUR dream and you can do anything you want with it. Using your imagination, you can rewrite the dream story to suit you. For instance, if you encounter an obstacle in a dream, such as a high wall blocking your path, you can rewrite the ending. For instance, you could grow wings and fly over the wall. Yes, that's right! Dreams are like fairy tales and anything goes. Magic is one of the important characteristics of dreams, just as it is in myths and legends. That's why grown-ups think dreams are silly and senseless. They have lost their love of magic and make-believe or imaginative play. A dream is simply another reality with a language, characteristics, and rules all its own.

The use of imagination in problem-solving as it occurs in magical dream solutions can help you become a more creative problem-solver in waking life. Through auto-suggestion you can learn to deal with challenges that come up in dreams, especially if they reappear often. Here is an example of how I solved a problem in a dream state. I had been having car problems in my dreams and decided, through auto-suggestion before falling asleep, that I would deal creatively with any problems that came up in my dreams. That night I dreamed the following:

> I've visited G. When I come out of her house I notice that the front right tire of my car is flat. I get very upset. Then I realize this is a dream and I can use magic. I conjure up a special bicycle pump and fill the tire with air. Then I drive to a gas station a few blocks away to have the tire fixed.

I felt very powerful, resourceful, and creative when I woke up from that dream. I had found a solution to my problem that worked beautifully given the context (the dream state) where magic is appropriate. I thought, if I can solve problems that well in my sleep, then I can certainly solve them in my waking state.

After you have reviewed your dream in your mind's eye, draw the key images that appeared. These might be people, animals, objects, places and scenes, symbolic forms, or other visual impressions that stand out. (See the drawing in the introduction to this chapter, page 136, for an example of a dream drawing.)

___

Write in free-association about the images you have drawn. What comes to mind when you look at each graphic image? What was its function in the dream? What qualities does it have (in the dream or in real life)? What qualities in yourself is it connected with? What do you feel or think about each image in your drawing?

___

Let the images in your dream drawing speak. Let them introduce themselves in the first person, present tense, and tell about themselves. You may want to respond and have a conversation. Write it all out as you would the script for a play.

___

Uses: This is an especially helpful technique for exploring fragmentary dreams, the ones you don't recall in detail but from which a few isolated images, events, or pieces of dialog emerge. Here, you can focus on the pieces of the puzzle you *do* remember. Putting your imagination to work through drawing and writing can help you de-code these symbols so you can find out what they mean to you personally at this time in your life.

I am a shell and a piece of earth — A shell IN a piece of earth. Rich fertile deep brown ruddy healthy soil of my life. Soil of my life. Shit of my life. The beauty is one with the ugliness. Can't have one w/out the other. A shell...

A mere outer covering. A beautiful home for an unseen inside. A protected inside.

From a dream where I found a beautiful shell in the earth.

Plate 76

146

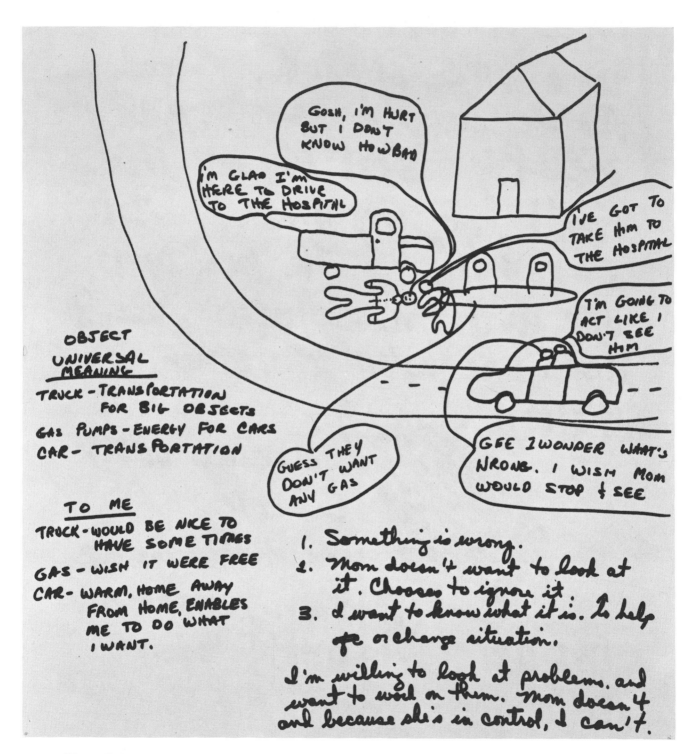

Plate 77

Use two pages side by side. On the first page, document your dream by writing it out. On the facing page, write down a "translation" into everyday terms connected with your life at the present time. Do this sentence by sentence, underlining the key words in both texts.

Uses: This method is intended to help you make a connection between the dream story and your current life situation. With practice, you will become more skilled at finding the hidden messages.

Example:

Dream: *Crossing the River*

It is *mid-day* and I am *walking* across a *large, flat meadow.*

As I walk I see a *beautiful woods* ahead *in the distance.*

As I get closer to the woods, I see *a river separating me from it.* There are *sharp rocks and rapids.*

I can't swim across (dangerous) and *I'm afraid to walk* for fear of falling from the rocks.

I decide to look up and down the river bank for a way across. I see a *bridge* (indicating that *others have solved this problem before me.*)

Meaning: *Entering a New Career*

I am *middle-aged* and steadily *moving foreward.* I have *lots of freedom now.*

I see a *new career as a writer ahead.* (Being in the woods always inspires me to write.)
There are *obstacles in the way*, keeping me from my goal of becoming a profess-ional writer.

I'm afraid of failure given my present financial resources and conditions. Survival needs must be met.

However, *I'm determined to reach my goal* of writing professionally. I need to research my first writing project and *structure the work*, set specific goal and schedules. I may *need advice from experienced writers,* too.

Plate 78

INTUITIONS AND HUNCHES

Pay attention to your intuitions and hunches and write them down when you have them. Sometimes these come through as premonitions and E.S.P. experiences: when you *know* something has happened or is going to occur before you actually have the physical "proof" or factual information.

Check your intuitions and hunches out whenever you can to see if they were indeed connected with actual physical events.

Variation: Review in your memory any E.S.P. or premonitional experiences you've had in your life. This includes pre-cognitive dreams (when you dream something that is happening at the time or happens later). Write these experiences down in your journal.

Uses: This is a way of learning to pay attention to and develop your intuitive powers. Since intuition is an important part of the creative process, this is also a means of enhancing your creativity. Intuition is a form of knowing which does not follow rational, logical ordering. It is imaginative and is used in free-association and "brain-storming" techniques where the mind is at play and anything goes. In using intuitive processes you can leap over the walls of the limitations inherent in exclusively rational thought. It is with intuition that you can get out of ruts and make creative breakthroughs. This is how revolutionary new ideas, discoveries, and inventions are born. But intuitions, like dreams, are often seen by our rationalistic minds as senseless and are dismissed on that account. We belittle an intuition, calling it "only a hunch," and therefore not to be taken too seriously. I encourage you to take your hunches and intuitions very seriously. They contain some of your highest, most profound insights and wisdom.

I've learned an expensive lesson about listening to my intuition and hunches. It's official, the money D. and I invested this summer is lost. All $4,600 of it is down the tubes.

The whole mess has been very painful for me. I've cursed myself so many times for not listening to my intuition.

At the time the investment deal was proposed to me I was under considerable stress. I reacted to the emotional appeal of D. rather than stepping back and listening with my inner voice. A week after I agreed to the investment I began having doubts, but then it was too late. I didn't know then how to appeal effectively to D. in order to get back our money.

The loss of the money has caused great financial hardships for me. It was all the savings I had. One thing is certain: never again will I allow myself to get swept away with get rich quick schemes. From this day forth I vow myself to pay close attention to my intuition and follow it even if I can't always explain why I feel the way I do.

Plate 79

THE GUIDE WITHIN ME

Get into a relaxed, meditative state with eyes closed. Then imagine yourself in a beautiful place. It might be a room, a place in nature. Wherever it is, let the beautiful environment form around you in your imagination. See it in your mind's eye, feel the experience of being there. Look around you and take it all in.

Still keeping your eyes closed and being in your beautiful environment, let an image appear before you. This might be a person, animal, object. Observe the image and notice its appearance in detail. Experience its presence. Then let the image speak to you. Ask its name and why it is appearing. Tell the image what you think and feel about it and what you want from it (assistance, advice, a gift of some kind). Then ask the image what it wants from you and for you. This image is your inner guide, the wisdom within you which is being personified or embodied through imagery. After you have conversed with your guide, thank it and release it to dissolve back into the beautiful environment. Then slowly let the environment fade and say goodbye, knowing that you can come back whenever you wish.

Write out your conversation with your guide. You may want to do this as a right/left hand dialog. Let your guide speak with your sub-dominant hand and respond with your dominant hand. Writing with the sub-dominant hand is optional in this exercise.

Uses: This exercise is intended to help you contact your own wisdom that lies hidden within. Often, we search for gurus and advisors in the outer world, hoping they will furnish us with answers to our problems. It is easy to ignore our own inner resources, the wise spirit or higher self that resides within us.

Here is one woman's dialog with two of her wisdom guides, the Snake Woman and John, the Healer.

Snake Woman, please help me. I'm feeling inundated and overwhelmed.

S.W.   These issues (problems) are a test for you—to be true to yourself and your innermost convictions. God is guiding your path. It is not in your control. It is not known to you! You are being brought into a new place and the doors that will open to you are full of surprises. John, the Healer, is important to you at this juncture. He is used to many trails in the wilderness-above and below ground. He will not abandon you. He is able to walk in the dark—he is not fearful. All is transitory.

John, help me with this confused, dark, crazy problem, please?

J.H.   Jane, come. I am not able to save you from the pain when you hurt. I will assure you, it won't last long. Your *anxiety* is what you are lost and entangled in now. Come on out and look at the long view—the mountain ranges. You must look at the distance instead of the mire.

Plate 80

LETTERS TO OTHERS

Sometimes letters contain important statements about the letter-writer's life. Your letters are worth keeping as a record of your life at a given point in time. A letter can also be an important tool in clarifying thoughts, feelings, wishes about yourself as well as about the person to whom the letter is written.

Not all letters to others need to be sent. In some situations, a "private" letter written in your journal can help you understand and formulate your inner response to the other person in a relationship. In this way you can sort things out and perhaps become clearer about your feelings. Of course, you may decide to share the feelings face to face. In this instance, the private journal letter serves as a preparation ground for more direct and effective communication. You may even want to give a copy of all or part of the letter to the other individual.

Uses: This is a means of documenting your own personal history as you live it. It is also a tool for clarifying relationships and promoting better communication.

"I hope I shall be able to confide in you completely, as I have never been able to do in anyone before, and I hope that you will be a great support and comfort to me."

Anne Frank 12 June 1942
to her imaginary friend Kitty
in *The Diary of Anne Frank*

. . . And in the past few months, being ill, being uninvolved with any lover or job commitment or anything that I could escape into or distract myself with, I've had to face myself—what do I want for me? I wrote a line in my journal: "As much as I love sunshine, I know that without rain there would be no rainbows and rainbows are what I came on this earth to create." So I have found meaning in all the pain and terror and confusion of the past 5 years—it was part of growing up . . . of becoming a deeper, fuller, more compassionate me. I don't think people who have never had the guts to feel their own pain and terror can really be compassionate, loving human beings. I know I could not really be truly intimate with others' pain until I had my own and felt it, and to be in touch with another person's pain is perhaps the door to loving. And it's closed to most people. They can "love" the lightness and superficiality in others—I could do that—but it was hard to *see* pain hiding behind anger, frustrations, reserve, let alone reach out to the person inside of it.

You did that for me—you reached behind the curtain of words (empty) and reasons and explanations and touched me in a very special way. It hurt. God it hurt like hell. (I can still feel what it felt like and it still makes me cry). It was like major surgery, like giving birth . . . .

Thank you for making this letter happen and for "seeing" the real me. You can only see what you already have within you.

I love you,
even when you don't love yourself.

L.

Plate 81

In luminous flashes of inner vision, we may discover jewels of wisdom hidden within ourselves. These flashes might come in words (a powerful phrase or poem) or in a glowing visual image or both. When these insights reveal themselves to us, it is as if veils of mist simply dropped away. Universal and timeless truths seem to emerge from the shadows and stand bathed in the light of deep understanding.

These are magic moments of inspiration and cannot be forced or programmed to happen. When they do occur, they are worth drawing or writing down as records of creative peak experiences that so enrich our lives.

To be free
is
to value
all that
I am proud of
and
all that
I am ashamed of
in myself
and
to accept
the whole
as
Being
me

Plate 82

COMPASSION...
needs pain as a teacher

12-6-76 1P.M.

Plate 83

Plate 84

"Any path is only a path, and there is no affront to oneself or to others, in dropping it if that is what your heart tells you . . . Look at every path closely and deliberately. Try it as many times as you think necessary. Then ask yourself, and yourself alone, one question . . . Does this path have a heart? If it does, the path is good; if it doesn't it is of no use."

—Carlos Castaneda
The Teachings of Don Juan

"Hold fast to dreams, for if dreams die, life is a broken winged bird that cannot fly."

—Langston Hughes

7   Where You're Going

Now it's time to look into the future by exploring your wishes and fantasies. With the power of your imagination, you can design the blue-prints and lay the foundation for the days and years to come. You can choose where you really want to go and how you want to get there, creating the road-map for finding the unlimited buried treasure within: your own *dear self*.

This chapter is intended to help you:

- pay closer attention to your fondest wishes and fantasies
- apply your creativity to goal-setting for the future
- develop the power of imagination and visualization for achieving your goals
- confront obstacles in your path
- take responsibility for creating your own life and fulfillment

WHAT DO YOU WANT TO BE WHEN YOU GROW UP?

Go back into your early memories and ask yourself:

What did I want to be when I grew up?

Review the years from childhood and adolescence. Remember all the things you wanted to be, no matter how "far out" or silly it seems to you now. For example, young children sometimes want to be animals, mythical characters, and the like.

Using your sub-dominant hand, make a list of all your childhood and adolescent fantasies about what you wanted to be and do when you reached adulthood.

Read over your list, checking the fantasies that you actually did live out. You may not have made a career of your fantasy, but may have experienced it in some way. Then asterisk the items on your list that you did not live out or experience. Ask yourself why. Was there social pressure against it? Did you lose interest in it? Was it too "far out"?

Using your dominant hand, on the next page make a list of things you would like to do or experiences you would like to have during the rest of your life. Include qualities or skills you want to develop, things you want to accomplish, states of being you wish to experience. Then choose one item from your list and use it as the focus for the next exercise, *Making My Dreams Come True.*

Uses: This exercise encourages you to revive your child-like sense of make-believe and fantasy as a means for developing your creative imagination. This allows you to open new doors, examine areas of potentiality. To quote an old song: "If you don't have a dream, how're you going to have a dream come true?"

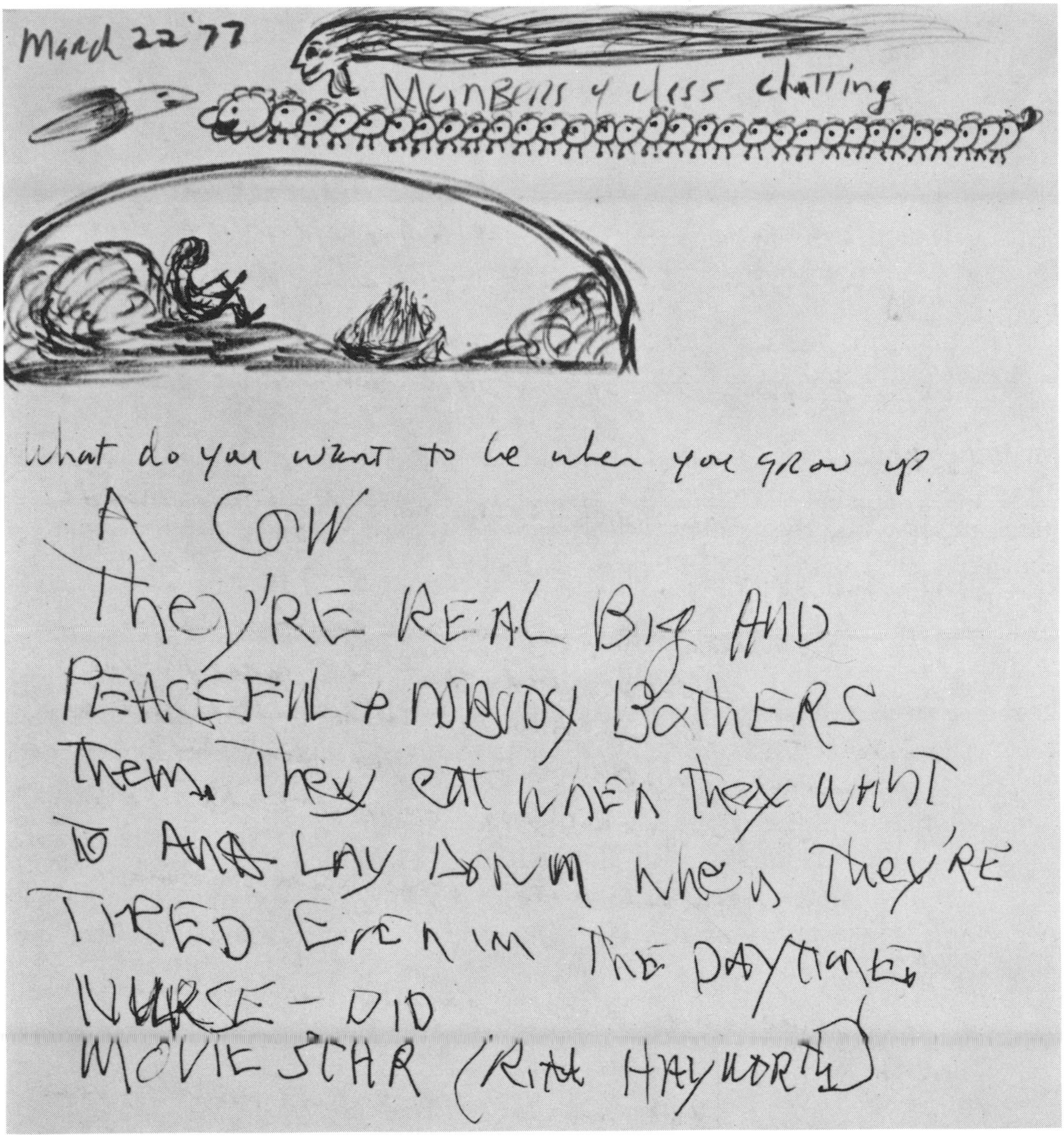

March 22 '77

MEMBERS 4 LESS chatting

what do you want to be when you grow up.

A COW
They're REAL Big AND
PEACEFUL + NOBODY BothERS
Them. They eat when they want
to AND LAY down when They're
TIRED EVEN IN The DAYTIME
NURSE – DID
MOVIE STAR (Rita HAYWORTH)

Plate 85

MAKING MY DREAMS COME TRUE

Focus on something you want to achieve or experience. Meditate upon it. Then divide the page for a three-part drawing, as follows:

1. How you see yourself now in relation to your goal or wish
2. The challenges or obstacles (within and without) blocking you
3. How you will see yourself after attaining your goal

Note: Draw sections 1 and 3 first, then go back and draw the obstacles in section 2.

Study your drawing of the obstacles. Let them talk to you and write it out on a new page.

Meditate regularly on drawing #3 so that the projection of how you will be after attaining your goal is etched into your mind. You can accompany these image-meditations with other fantasies having to do with the successful achievement of your goal.

Uses: In this exercise, you are setting goals, examining blocks, and visualizing success. Each step is crucial. It's a way to assess where you're at and where you want to be. Dealing with the obstacles in the way helps you to systematically pull out the weeds that are choking the growth of your true potential. Meditating upon the desired goal in which you feel it *as if* it had already happened is a powerful tool for realizing your dreams. It is a form of auto-suggestion which works through imagery and fantasy from the creative imagination.

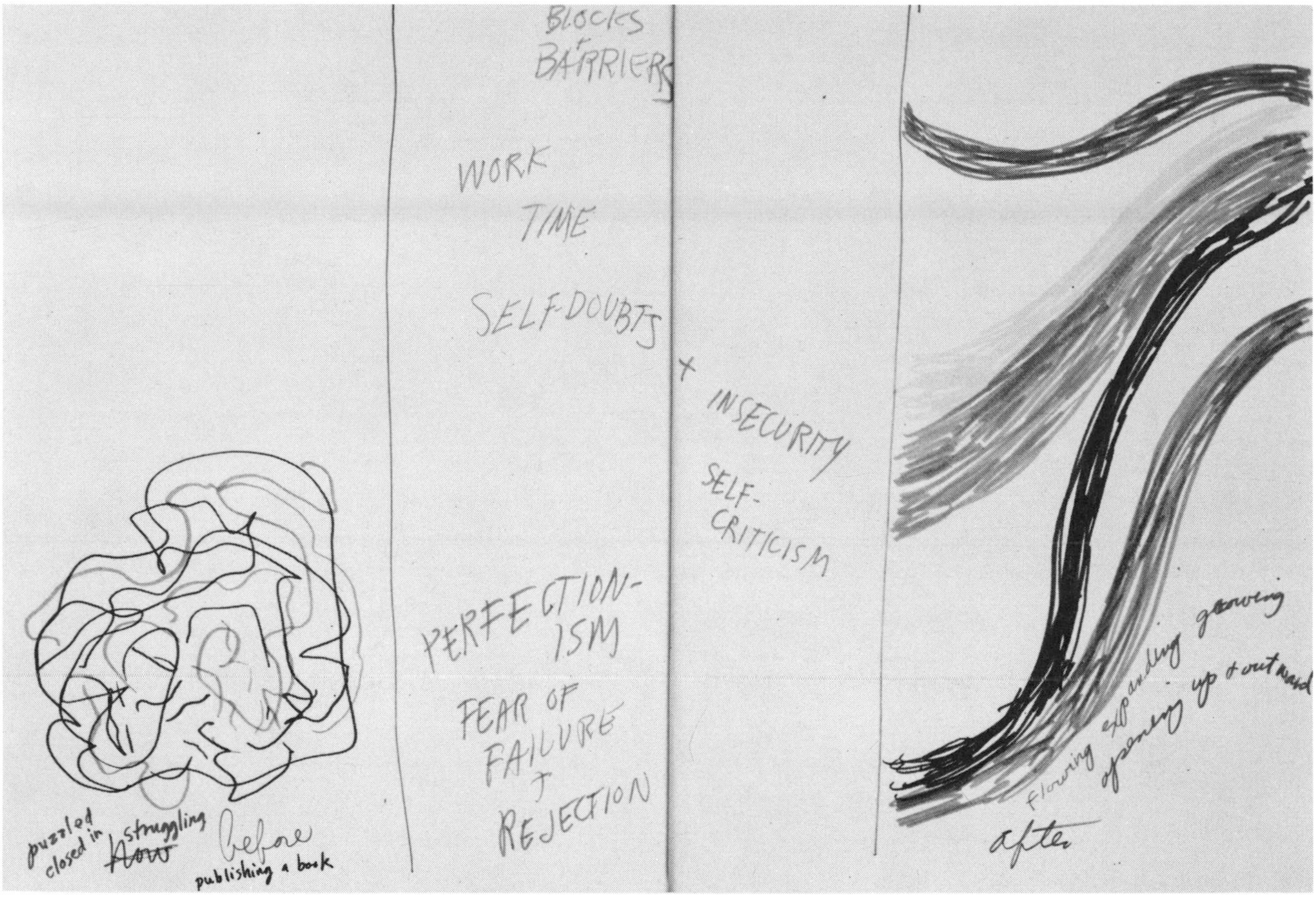

BLOCKS + BARRIERS

WORK
TIME
SELF-DOUBTS
+ INSECURITY
SELF-CRITICISM

PERFECTION-ISM
FEAR OF FAILURE + REJECTION

puzzled closed in struggling before
publishing a book

flowing expanding growing
opening up + outward
after

Plate 86

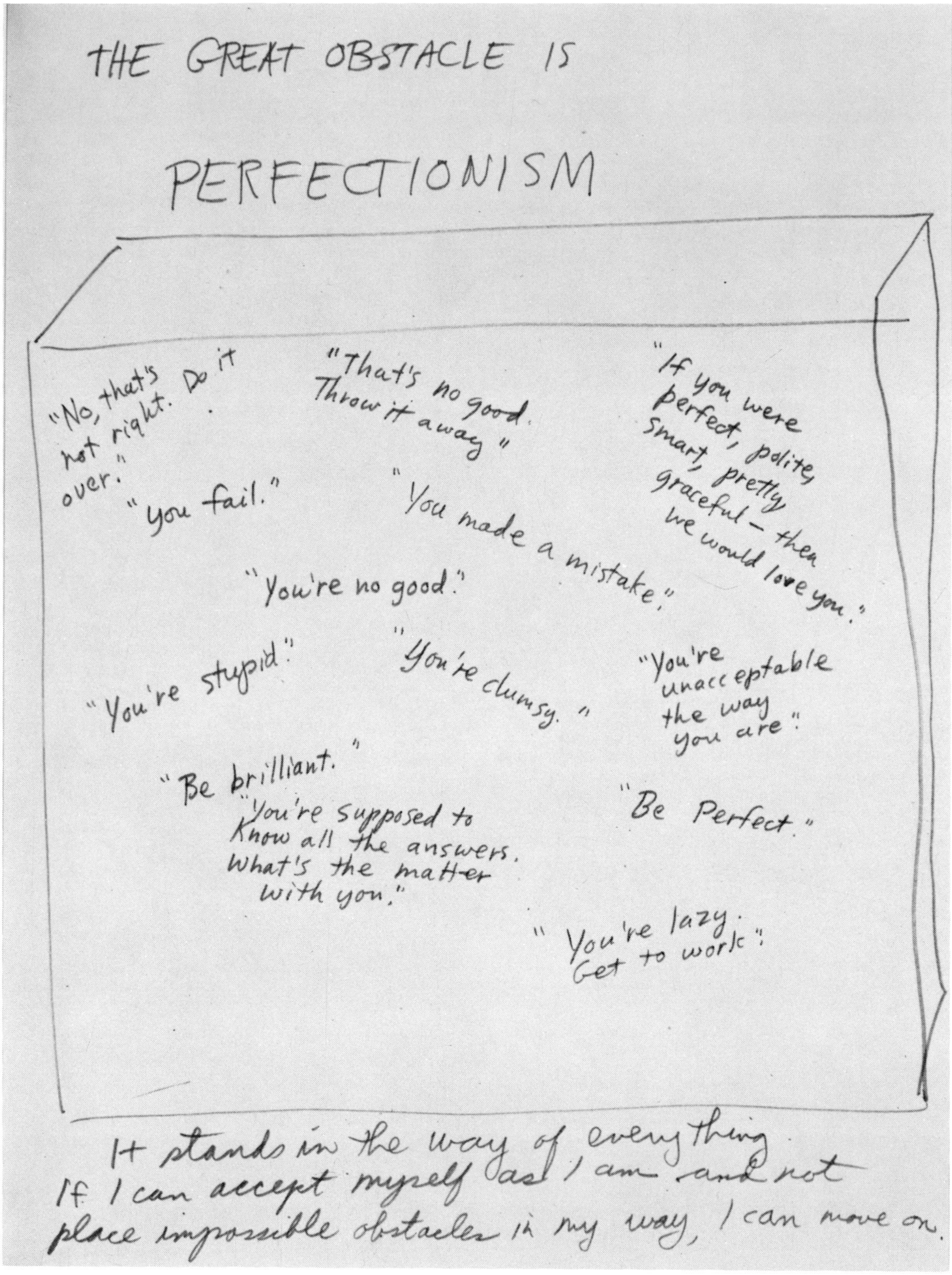

THE GREAT OBSTACLE IS

PERFECTIONISM

"No, that's not right. Do it over."

"That's no good. Throw it away."

"If you were perfect, polite, smart, pretty, graceful — then we would love you."

"You fail."

"You made a mistake."

"You're no good."

"You're stupid."

"You're clumsy."

"You're unacceptable the way you are."

"Be brilliant."

"You're supposed to know all the answers. What's the matter with you."

"Be Perfect."

"You're lazy. Get to work."

It stands in the way of everything. If I can accept myself as I am and not place impossible obstacles in my way, I can move on.

Plate 87

I WISH

Imagine that you have been given the wherewithal (resources, time, money) to have any wish. What would it be? Write it out.

Write a poem entitled: "I Wish . . ." Do not be concerned with meter or rhyme. Just let the words flow out naturally.

Uses: This exercise is a means of stretching your imagination, for seeing beyond some of the self-imposed limitations which shrink your vision and aspirations.

Being

I wish
　I Were
　　But I Am.
　　　And Always Shall Be.
　　　　(Always?) How can I
　　Presume the Always?
　　　But Yes, my Essence
　　　　Mingles with Those of Eons Past
　　　　　and Eons More to Come
Forms an ENDLESS CHAIN
　　　of
ALWAYS Stretching Out past
　　Barriers of Time and Space
　　　Yet condensing into a drop of dew
　　on the face
　　of the budding Babe
　　　Miniscule, Infinite,
Broad, Delicate
　　Finer than a Hair, more forceful
More force than a hammer-sledge
　　Containing all that Ever Was, or
　　　Ever Shall Be
Condensing into a Single Cell—Me.

Plate 88

WHERE I'LL BE IN FIVE YEARS

Close your eyes and go through a typical day in your life at the present time. Visualize yourself waking up in the morning and go through the day's activities. Picture the environments you move through, the people you encounter.

Now, imagine a typical day *five years from now*. Visualize yourself waking up in the morning, picture the environment, imagine going through the day's activities. Imagine the people you encounter, the various places you go, and how you feel about your life style. Write out a brief description of your imaginary day five years into the future. Write it in the present tense as if it is happening now.

Repeat the five year projection, but this time imagine you are a member of the opposite sex. Write about it.

Look over your three visualizations and see if there were any major differences. Between past and present? Between male and female? Write the comparisons down, then ask yourself:

> *What am I already doing that will get me where I want to be in five years?*
> *What other things can I do to get me where I want to be?*

Write down all of your thoughts on these questions.

Variation: This exercise can be based on any time period that feels appropriate to you. You might want to try it as a one year projection or even less.

Uses: This is a tool for opening up your ability to fantasize into the future. It is a way to realize that you create your own life just as an artist creates a painting. You can play with various options in your imagination and then choose which direction you want to go. If you clarify what you really want, then it's easier to take the next step, such as developing the skills, resources, and attitudes necessary to achieve your goals.

Note: This exercise was based on a technique used in Future Focus workshops developed by Social Engineering Technology in Los Angeles, California.

". . . it is as though my eyes were seeing farther than usual—as though the dimming walls of the cramped little room were betaking themselves away—as though today I were permitted to take a look into the future."

—Ranier Maria Rilke

"Imagination is the beginning of creation: You imagine what you desire; you will what you imagine; and at last you create what you will."

—George Bernard Shaw

Close your eyes and imagine that you are standing in front of a series of doors. Create a setting (inside or outside) for these doors. Each door is different: each one represents an opportunity or challenge in your life. Visualize each door. See its color, shape, size, and decoration, symbol or sign appearing on it. Open each door and see what's behind it.

Draw the doors and on each one draw a symbol, color or write a word that expresses what you found behind the door.

Draw another picture that shows what you found behind the doors. Then write about it.

Uses: This is a tool for further developing your creative imagination through fantasy and visualization. It can help you reveal more of your deepest dreams, fondest wishes and major concerns. It can expand your vision of some possible directions for the future and broaden your choices.

Plate 89A

Plate 89B

As I closed my eyes I was in an open-air rectangular courtyard with doors surrounding me, similar to a cloister I once visited. All the doors were wood-slat and smaller than ones of today. It was a peaceful setting. *One door* had a beautiful gold door knob and another had a symbol. When instructed to open the doors of the future, the first was the one with the gold doorknob. Inside was a village with off-white houses and tiled roofs stretching up a green hillside overlooking a bay of the Mediterranean. *The second door* was plain but when I opened it a white knight on a powerful white horse towered over me. I quickly shut the door. *The third door* had the symbol (which we found out later is an ankh) and inside was a hazy picture of a man and woman at the end of a brick pathway amidst the green lushness of nature while sunlight streamed through the trees.

How it might relate to me:

The first door was a place I wanted to live which represented my desire to leave this widespread city and move to a community of fewer people but more richness in beauty and spirit.

The second, being the knight and horse, frightened me. Not that they might harm me but the power, especially in the horse, overwhelmed me. The horse was a muscular and beautiful creature with intense strength. Many things could relate to me in this image but one I was positive of: I was the horse, strong-willed, and the white knight was my father restraining me, controlling me for his own needs. And now that I'm no longer "under" him, I'm controlling myself and afraid to face or unleash my true self—always trying to be perfect.

The last door with the ankh symbol was strange for I had no idea when I saw the symbol what it stood for. Also, the image was hazy where the first two were sharp and alive. The couple, hand in hand, looking into each other's eyes, represented to me that there was a deeper love to feel but it was off in the future. Which relates to my marriage as I'm in the process of breaking down the picture-perfect facade and delving for a deeper communal love between a man and woman. The ankh is an Egyptian symbol for life. The connection to me was that the key to life is love.

Plate 89C

BUILDING MY DREAM HOUSE

Imagine that you have been given the resources to build the house of your dreams. You can select any location, style of architecture, materials. Close your eyes and imagine where your dream house is situated, what it is like. Take an imaginary walk through and around it, visualizing it as clearly as you can.

Draw a floorplan of your dream house. Indicate the color and atmosphere or function of each area in any way you wish. Include entrances and windows and any part of the immediate environmental setting you wish.

Study your floorplan over. Consider it as a blue-print of your emerging self, priorities, self-image, wishes for the future. What does the floorplan say about you? Write it down.

Variation: Draw pictures of your dream house as you might actually see it; details of certain areas, highlights, spaces that are most important to you.

Uses: This is an exercise in building a new perception of yourself through designing an outward expression. A house can be seen as a symbol of the self, illustrating again that your life is your own creation, your personal work of art.

Imagine something you would like to accomplish or experience, a state of being you would like to attain. Imagine that *it has already happened.* Then visualize yourself telling someone about it in the past tense, as an accomplished fact.

Write down what you said to the other person in your imaginary conversation.

Uses: This is a technique in applied creative imagination with the aim of establishing the attitude necessary for actualizing your wish, for increasing your faith in your ability to achieve your goals.

March 25, 1977

Imaginary letter (after my book is published)

Dear B.:

Well, it's happened. The book is published. I can hardly believe it. I got a copy in the mail today.

It's gorgeous. I wept when I opened it. Three years in the making. Three years since I started the workshops that led to this. No, really it was four years—for it was then that I started my own journal.

Well, you saw me through a lot of craziness. I remember sitting with you in my living room after I'd been to a local publisher. I cried. And, of course, we talked about whether I was a "writer" or not.

Anyway, I want to thank you for your continued support and your gorgeous examples for the book. They are so perfect. Wait until you see them. "Bring on the scratch paper," indeed!

Love, L.

Plate 90

TREASURE MAP

Close your eyes and ask:

> *What is my buried treasure? What are the qualities or states of being that lie hidden within me as potentiality?*

Visualize your buried treasure in some kind of imagery. Meditate upon it.

Draw an image of your buried treasure. Then draw a map with a path leading to that treasure. The path is your life. Show the obstacles (blocks, hindrances) and the helpers (guides, resources, assistance) you have encountered along the way. Label these if you wish.

Have a conversation with the obstacles and then with the helpers. Write your conversation down.

Uses: This is an excellent exercise for further exploring your latent talents, abilities, wishes. It can help you confront your limitations and make use of your resources toward reaching your goals. This is the secret of Creative Journalkeeping. It is a journey through the path of outer expression to find the inner unfolding self. It is a never-ending process, for there will always be more potential to discover, more buried treasures to find.

TREASURE MAP

Buried treasure
glowing bright
will you ever
know the light?

Treasure-seeker
come and find me
any map will do.

the treasure — my whole Self

Self doubt Bog & Swamp

Lady in the mist Lights the way

Worthless hot Springs

should Glacier Lake

Scarey mountains

Hidden valley Pass

Diane Points to Hidden valley Pass

HARRY is wilderness Guide Past should Lake & Worthless hot springs.

5-18-77

mary - Diane & Lucia Sing & encourage Past Self doubt Bog & Swamp.

Plate 91

WHERE I'M GOING

Ask yourself:

> *Where have I travelled within myself since I began the Creative Journal-keeping process? What have I learned? Where am I going from here?*

Meditate upon these questions for awhile.

Write down your feelings and thoughts about your journal journey. You might want to draw your observations in graphic imagery. Give yourself love and appreciation for venturing down the path to find your own *dear self*.

Uses: This is a means for giving yourself feedback about your growth process related to the work and play you have done in your journal using the exercises in this book. This is a retrospective glance back through the rearview mirror and a vision of the future which is there for you to discover and create.

"And now here is my secret, a very simple secret:

It is only with the heart that one can see rightly; what is essential is invisible to the eye."

—The fox
in *The Little Prince*
Antoine Saint Exupery

I hate to stop — it drives me so but now I feel I must let my pen go — to rest awhile to feel what I've done. To look back with all that's in me, to know what I've felt here and there — here and now — past and present. Living and breathing, in and out, the air goes through my nostrils and yet I don't feel alive at times – just existing. But I don't want to go on that word or that feeling. I've got a lot out but I've a lot to give so goodbye my book by living what I feel. You seem to take on a personality, book — how strange that I address you as a friend. But you indeed are but maybe in you, I'm being my own friend.

Thanks old pal — its been fun !!!

Plate 92

REVIEWING YOUR JOURNAL

An important feature of journal-keeping is that it provides you with a tangible, permanent record of your own growth: a rear-view mirror, so to speak. Looking back at where you've been can be very illuminating and can give you a new sense of perspective. It may reveal patterns that repeat themselves. Seeing your patterns or cycles opens you to choices and the possibility of alternatives. Sometimes, journal review can unearth some jewels of wisdom that got buried somehow. Often, when I am reviewing past volumes, I am surprised by the insightfulness I find there. My first reaction is: "Did I write that? I didn't know I knew that back then."

How to Review

I recommend reviewing the journal in any way you like. Some possibilities are as follows:

- read it to yourself aloud
- read it aloud, tape record it and play it back
- take slides of the art work and project them
- keep a summary log with dates and a synopsis of each entry in chronological order (see example on next page)

I keep a summary log in a separate three-ring folder. It helps me in doing a quick over-view and also in locating a particular period. I use it as an index or guide to my journal. I usually summarize the key experiences and feelings in my log. Some journal-keepers highlight feelings only (as in the example shown here), some log events. Do whatever feels right for you. No matter how you do it, reviewing your journal can make you aware of the vast resources you carry within you and that is what Creative Journal-keeping is all about.

	Sept. 1, 1977:	angry, pissed off, frustrated, powerless
	Sept. 6	disoriented, pissed off, sad, powerless, crazy, vulnerable, trapped
	Sept. 7	wonderful, excited joyful, happy
	Sept. 8	clear, confident
	Sept. 12	determined
	Sept. 14	sad, vulnerable, lonely, trapped
	Sept. 17	vulnerable, scared
	Sept. 20	scared, frightened, vulnerable, sad
	Sept. 23	inspired, supportive
	Sept. 26	under stress
	Oct. 2	introspective, strong
	Oct. 4	open, warm, tender
dream	*Oct. 9	introspective, quiet, calm
	Oct. 16	over-extended, stunned, cared for
	Oct. 17	introspective, resolved
	Oct. 18	worried, wounded
	Oct. 19	unclear, afraid, defensive, vulnerable
	Oct. 20	scared, kinetic, conflicted, open, tender
	Oct. 21	responsible
	Oct. 23	reflective
	Oct. 24	frustrated, tired
	Oct. 25	efficient, productive, clear
	Oct. 26	resolved, clear, sad, strong, capable
	Nov. 1	introspective, clear

Plate 93A

Nov. 1, 1977

By tomorrow I will have finished my fifth journal book. It seems fitting that the ending will coincide with the Day of the Dead. As I bring closure to these last entries I want to savor the moment.

Even though it is two months short of my annual ritual of recording a word or two of how I've felt each journal entry, I decided to re-read all the journals today. I felt like bringing closure to a chapter of my life in preparation for some new beginnings.

The process of recording all the entries was both draining and revealing. I'm glad I did it. I discovered some interesting stuff. It's evident to me that, since I've kept a journal, my recollection of events, feelings, and my dreams are much clearer in focus than any other time in my life.

I compared the journal entries from this year with last year. In 1976 the theme could be described as sad, lonely, angry, hostile, anxious, and afraid. This year I feel more open, expansive, vulnerable, clear, and much stronger. The movement out of the snake pit and into the light is definitely there. Being able to validate for myself that change is occuring is wonderful.

I noticed some patterns, too. I never realized it before, but often when I was feeling angry, a few days prior I was often feeling sad or lonely. I suspect that what happens is that to mask the vulnerable parts of me, my monster lashes out in the form of rage. That's an old pattern, one I'd like to transform into something more productive. I wonder what would happen if I allowed more people to see my vulnerability? I think I'll experiment with that notion.

Plate 93B

Post-script

As I prepared the final manuscript of this book, I realized how therapeutic it had been for me to write it. I had to struggle with all my demons throughout the process. It went something like this.

In early 1976, I decided to write a "how to" book on Creative Journal-keeping. I was inspired by the success of my classes and the enthusiastic encouragement of my students for such a book. But before I ever lifted pen to paper, I came down with a serious case of the "panics." A critical voice in my head said: "You're not a professional writer. You'll never get a book published."

Just then, I happened to meet a writer with a best-seller to his credit. He offered to co-author the book based on my journal classes. I thought I'd solved my problem. Actually, I see now that I was trying to avoid the real challenge: writing the book myself. The more we discussed the book, the clearer it became that the collaboration would not work. There were philosophical differences and personality clashes. So I dropped that idea and was thrown back once again onto my own resources.

How to begin? I decided to tape record my class presentations. I thought perhaps the book could simply be a series of transcriptions interspersed with examples from people's journals. But the first tape sounded terrible to me and it was even worse when I transcribed it to paper. Too wordy, unstructured. Too much discussion and questioning and answering for a book instruction. This would never do. No, taping the class did not seem to be the answer to writing the book.

However, listening to the tape was very helpful for improving my teaching. I used it as a tool for "cleaning up my act," as they say. For I began to really hear myself speak and use words. As a result, I started using words differently, more economically, articulating my thoughts more clearly. I felt much better about my teaching. But, "the book" was still sitting there as an idea, unwritten.

A few months went by during which I developed an advanced course in Creative Journal-keeping, and then a still more advanced course. More exercises, more experience in field-testing the material, more success in teaching. Still no book. It bothered me. I felt stuck. I knew what I wanted to do, but I wasn't doing it. The classic creative block.

Then a change occurred as if by magic. Around Christmas of 1976, almost a year after I had first decided to write the book, I resolved to *do it*. That was the key step: making the firm commitment to work on the book. It was an act of will. It enabled me to take the next step (setting up a writing schedule) and all the steps that followed from that. I set aside two to three days a week to work on the book exclusively. I would permit no interruptions. I decided to follow this schedule until the book was completed. I would not wait for an agent or publisher. I would go ahead and create the book.

But there were many obstacles ahead. There were days when the old demon of Self-Doubt would come to haunt me. Naturally, I used my own exercises to deal with this devilish villain. My inner dialog at the time appears on pages 92 and 93. I also reinforced my goal with positive images of how I would feel after I published my book (pages 161 and 171). And I scrutinized the major block: Perfectionism, page 162.

So I used the very content of the book I was writing to help me write the book. And it worked! In looking back, I realize that I was working as intensely on myself as I was on the book and, ironically, it took nine months from the time I began seriously working on the book on my own until I found its publisher. I was giving birth to the author in me.

God is within you.
Respect your Self
because He belongs to you.

If you understand your own true nature
you will know that you are God.

Look for everything within yourself.
Everything is inside you.
Increase and enhance this awareness;
Learn how to become ecstatic inside yourself.
The one you are looking for is you.
The one you want to atttain is you.

—Swami Muktananda

Supreme devotion is absolute
sacrifice to the path of the Self and
wanting to know the Truth.

—Gurumayi Chidvilasananda